HOME BIRTH RECORDS OF
DR. CHICHESTER TAPSCOTT PEIRCE
Revisited 1900-1919

Lancaster, Richmond and Northumberland Counties in Virginia

Margaret L. Forrester
and
Deborah Beuchelt Walker

**Northumberland
Historical Press**
NHP

Northumberland Historical Press
Heathsville, Virginia

Front Cover: Family photographs from the personal collection of Margaret L. Forrester.

ISBN: 978-1-957928-35-7
Library of Congress Control Number: 2023905216

Printed in the United States of America

PREFACE

Four years ago in 2018, I published a book, which recorded the home births attended by Dr. Chichester Tapscott Peirce from November of 1919 to August of 1954. The title of that book is *Home Birth Records of Dr. Chichester Tapscott Peirce 1919-1954, Lancaster, Richmond, and Northumberland Counties in Virginia.* The source for these records was 30 small books entitled *Physician's Bedside Birth Records,* compliments of the Bureau of Vital Statistics, State Department of Health, Richmond, Virginia. Within these books and also on paper pill envelopes, Dr. Peirce recorded some 1400 home births attended by him.

After the publication of this book, I kept thinking of the early years of Dr. Peirce's practice: 1900 to 1919. As stated in the preface of the book noted above, there did not appear to be any records of home births kept by Dr. Peirce during this period (a fact proven to be incorrect by statements to the contrary on several of the early birth certificates). Therefore, my dear friend and fellow genealogist, Deborah Beuchelt Walker, and I set out to try and find these birth records for Lancaster, Northumberland, and Richmond Counties on the Northern Neck of Virginia. Our search was for actual birth certificates with Dr. Peirce's signature on them from 1900 to 1919.

To begin this process, Mrs. Walker and I searched existing cemetery records for local cemeteries in the three counties for gravesites with births recorded between 1900 and 1919.[1] These cemeteries were in the area of the Northern Neck where Dr. Peirce practiced medicine (upper Lancaster County, upper Northumberland County and lower Richmond County with most of his practice being in Lancaster County).

Enter Ancestry.com! After making lists of these gravesites from over 33 churches, we then went to Ancestry.com to try and find the birth certificates with Dr. Peirce's signature on them. Later in our research, we discovered that now one can access Ancestry's website, type in a date (1910 for example), and the location (Lancaster County, VA for example) and up comes all records for Lancaster County for that year. With a few more clicks, one can see just the

---

[1] These records included the books *In Remembrance...* by Margaret L. Hill and Clyde H. Ratcliffe, pub. 2002; *The Shepherd's Fold...*The Genealogical Society of the Northern Neck, pub. 2012, and *Precious Memories in Oakland Cemetery Echoes from Mulch, Virginia* by Helen and Charles Burgess, pub. 2016. Findagrave.com was also searched.

birth records, with the majority of them having images of the actual birth certificates, each with the doctor's signature (in our case, that of Dr. Peirce).

Over a period of about two years, Mrs. Walker and I have searched all the birth certificates on Ancestry.com year by year from 1900 to 1919 in each of the three counties named above and have found 252 more home birth records, bringing the total number of records in both books to 1,652 births attended by Dr. Peirce.

As the early Dr. Peirce records were found, the signatures of many other physicians kept coming up on home births attended by them. Therefore, a list of these doctors from all three counties is included in this book. The organizational meeting of the Northern Neck Medical Association (NNMA) was held in Heathsville in 1904[2] and many of the doctors from the surrounding counties attended. A picture of some of them is included in this book. The names of the doctors who attended this first meeting of the NNMA are listed under the photo; however, they are not listed as they are seated in the photo.

Also, many of these birth certificates display the names and residences of midwives who attended these early home births. Included is a list of these capable, caring women from all three counties for the years 1900 to 1919.

All records of home births (attended by both doctors and midwives) had to be submitted to the county registrars to be officially recorded. These registrars' names also appeared on the birth certificates. Therefore, there is a list of these officials as well for all three counties. In the case of a delayed birth certificate, the document was signed by state registrars whose names are also listed. This list is again for the years 1900 to 1919.

The home birth information included in this book came from copies of original birth certificates or delayed birth certificates as found on Ancestry.com. A delayed birth certificate was usually applied for by the individual whose birth occurred prior to 1912, the first year birth certificates were required by the state of Virginia. Most of the delayed birth certificates in this book are dated in the 1940s and 1950s when proof of birth was required for such things as military service, marriage licenses, jobs, or a Social Security number. Proof of birth for these delayed certificates included such sources as family Bible records, baptism records, baby books, Federal Census records, and statements by other family members or neighbors. My personal favorite was recorded by the mother of an individual who stated, "I was there!" Also on several of these delayed birth certificates is a statement that the proof of birth was taken from the doctor's personal records (in our research, Dr. Peirce). Many delayed birth certificates did not have the doctor's signature.

---

[2] *Northern Neck News,* edition and year not given.

However, Mrs. Walker and I have found the ones with Dr. Peirce's signature on them.

I have included examples of three images, two of original birth certificates and one of a delayed birth certificate, which the reader can see following the preface. The information in all of the home births abstracted in this book comes from birth certificates similar to these three images.

The records in this book are abstracted from the birth certificates and include:

- Location of Birth (county, district, and town if given)
- Full Name of Child (if given)
- Date of Birth
- Father's Name, Age, Occupation, and Race
- Mother's Maiden Name, Age, and Race
- Original vs. Delayed Birth Certificate

The birth records are divided by county for Lancaster, Northumberland, and Richmond Counties, and listed alphabetically within each county.

Deborah Walker and I both hope the reader enjoys reading this book and perhaps can now find more relatives who were brought into this world by Dr. C. T. Peirce.

Margaret L. Forrester
March 2023

**An Example of an Original Birth Certificate
Signed by Dr. Peirce (1913)**

Source: Ancestry.com, *Virginia, U.S., Birth Records, 1912-2015, Delayed Birth Records, 1721-1920.*

Another Example of an Original Birth Certificate
Signed by Dr. Peirce (1917)

Source: Ancestry.com, *Virginia, U.S., Birth Records, 1912-2015, Delayed Birth Records, 1721-1920.*

**Copy of a Delayed Birth Certificate
with the Date of Birth January 15, 1900 and the
State Registrar's File Date of November 20, 1945**

ORGANIZATIONAL MEETING—Of the Northern Neck Medical Society was held in Heathsville in 1904 and a majority of the group sat for the photograph shown above. Not all of the above group can be identified, nor can the two men seated in chairs on the porch and young boy seated on the third row. The members of the Society present for the organizational meeting were: Drs. J. W. Tankard, M. M. Walker, F. W. Lewis, L. E. Cockrell, W. N. Chinn, R. F. Eubank, A. C. Fisher, M. C. Oldham, H. W. Harding, W. C. Chowning, C. T. Peirce, B. A. Middleton, J. A. Rice, L. G. Mitchell, A. N. Brent, R. E. Booker, H. L. Segar, R. H. Stuart, R. O. Lyell. The News especially thanks Mrs. Robert Harris of Kinsale for sharing this photo and one of Dr. Cockrell's first automobile with us and our Reedville correspondent, Mr. Edward Earle, for calling them to our attention.

**Organizational Meeting of the
Northern Neck Medical Association, 1904**

Source: Northumberland County Historical Society Files,
undated newspaper clipping from the *Northern Neck News.*

CONTENTS

PRACTICING PHYSICIANS ON VIRGINIA'S NORTHERN NECK

Lancaster, Northumberland and Richmond Counties

1900 to 1919

In researching Dr. C. T. Peirce's home births from 1900 to 1919, we found birth certificates from Lancaster County, Northumberland County, and Richmond County (all counties where Dr. Peirce practiced medicine).[3] Many of the birth certificates were signed by physicians other than Dr. Peirce. The list that follows names those physicians, the location of their practices (as written on the actual birth certificates) and their birth and death dates.[4] The reader can now see many of the physicians who were attending home births in the above-named Virginia counties between the years 1900 and 1919, the focus dates for this research.

LANCASTER COUNTY, VIRGINIA

Dr. Samuel Downing, Lancaster, VA, 1892-1937

Dr. Henry Jeter Edmonds, Kilmarnock, VA, 8/14/1866-12/13/1934

Dr. Horace Taylor Hawkins, Irvington, VA, 12/12/1887-7/30/1942

Dr. Benjamin Henry Bascom Hubbard, White Stone, VA, 1873-1940

Dr. Frank Waring Lewis, Morattico, VA, 5/28/1857-2/14/1928

Dr. William Jeffries Newbill Irvington, VA, 12/17/1846-12/15/1930

Dr. Morgan E. Norris, Kilmarnock, VA, 8/13/1888-5/18/1966

Dr. Maryus Curtis Oldham, Lancaster, VA, 9/20/1881-2/27/1946

Dr. Chichester Tapscott Peirce, Lively, VA, 11/22/1877-9/6/1964

Dr. George Hume Steuart, Ottoman, VA, 4/10/1865-1/6/1945

---

[3] Source for all images of birth certificates is *Ancestry.com, Virginia, U.S., Birth Records, 1912-2015, Delayed Birth Records, 1721-1920*, accessed 2021-2022.
[4] Findagrave.com and *In Remembrance…*Hill & Ratcliff.

NORTHUMBERLAND COUNTY, VIRGINIA

Dr. John Rockwell Atwell Wicomico Church, VA, 1884-9/11/1927

Dr. Robert Eubank Booker, Lottsburg, VA, 8/13/1880-2/25/1963

Dr. Andrew Mason Brent, Heathsville, VA, 10/2/1856-12/24/1926

Dr. Loren Eugene Cockrell, Reedville, VA, 5/5/1870-11/15/1957

Dr. Richard Llewellyn Hudnall, Lilian, VA, 10/4/1877-4/5/1959

Dr. James Adolphus Rice, Heathsville, VA, 10/1/1866-11/18/1924

Dr. Samuel Enoch Weymouth, Callao, VA, 1/5/1877-3/26/1973

RICHMOND COUNTY, VIRGINIA

Dr. Andrew Caswell Fisher, Emmerton, VA, 1/26/1852-2/7/1922

Dr. John Hampton Hare, Newland, VA, 10/16/1884-4/19/1954[5]

Dr. H. Roland Lickle, Farnham, VA, 1888-1939

Dr. Vernon Leslie Litsinger, Farnham, VA, 2/4/1884-10/14/1941

Dr. Robert Oliver/Olliver Lyell, Warsaw, VA, 7/14/1878-2/29/1968

Dr. Benjamin Arthur Middleton, Emmerton, VA. 3/6/1856-4/2/1933

Dr. Henry Launcelot Segar, Warsaw, VA, 3/21/1869-3/6/1954

WESTMORELAND COUNTY, VIRGINIA

Dr. Walter Neale Chinn, Hague, VA, 12/30/1871-6/28/1949

Dr. Percy Everett Schools, Montross, VA, 9/6/1888-8/24/1963

Dr. Harry Marbury Tayloe, Hague, VA, 11/14/1874-4/21/1927

Physicians whose names are on local birth certificates but with no Northern Neck birth or death dates that could be found by this researcher:

Dr. J. Strubinsky	Edwardsville, VA
Dr. E. Gordon Valk	Tangier Island and Bundick, VA (two different birth certificates)

---

[5] Dr. Hare's obituary can be found in the *United States Deceased Physicians File (AMA) 1864-1968* and in a 1954 *Richmond, VA News-Leader* newspaper as follows: "Hare, John Hampton, Warsaw, VA.; Maryland Medical College, Baltimore, 1905; served during World War I; died in Richmond April 19 [1954]; aged 69." Source: familysearch.org.

MIDWIVES OF THE
NORTHERN NECK OF VIRGINIA
1900-1919

In the years 1900 to 1919 on which this research focuses, many families, both African American and Caucasian, used the services of midwives when it came time to deliver their babies. The midwives themselves were both African American and Caucasian women. The midwives had guidelines from the state of Virginia, which they had to follow when delivering the babies and reporting the births afterwards.[6]

In this search for babies delivered by Dr. C. T. Peirce of Lancaster County, Virginia, this researcher came across many of these midwives' names on birth certificates from the Northern Neck.[7]

Listed below are the names of over one hundred midwives and their residences as they appear on many birth certificates dated between 1900 and 1919 in Lancaster, Northumberland, and Richmond Counties with one from Essex County and five from Westmoreland County:

ESSEX COUNTY, VIRGINIA

Miss/Mrs. Bundy   Mt. Landing, VA

LANCASTER COUNTY, VIRGINIA

Emily Ball   Brookvale, VA

Maria Blackwell   Weems, VA

Massby Boyd   Nuttsville, VA

Jane Coleman   Merry Point, VA

---

[6] Claudine Curry Smith and Mildred H. B. Roberson, *My Bag Was Always Packed The Life and Times of a Virginia Midwife*; published by First Books Library, 2003.

[7] Source for all images of birth certificates is Ancestry.com, *Virginia, U.S., Birth Records, 1912-2015, Delayed Birth Records, 1721-1920*, accessed 2021-2022.

Leanna Coleman	White Stone, VA
Mary J. Corbin	Mollusk, VA
Charlotte Davenport	Lancaster Courthouse, VA
Ellen Dixon	Merry Point, VA
Willie Gibson	Merry Point, VA
Adline/Adeline Greene	Weems, VA
Julia Hammonds	Mollusk, VA
Ann Harcum	Kilmarnock, VA
Susan Harcum	Kilmarnock, VA
Olidia Bell Haydon	Senora, VA
Elsie Henderson	Boer, VA (near Mollusk, VA)
Anne Jackson	Nuttsville, VA
Eliza Jones	White Stone, VA
Morgent/Margaret Luster	Kilmarnock, VA
Emeline McCoy	Merry Point, VA
Annette/Arnette Morris	Kilmarnock, VA
Eliza Pinn	Palmer, VA
Angeline Smith	Kilmarnock, VA
Mary Thomas	Boer, VA (near Mollusk, VA)
Sallie Thomas	Litwalton, VA
Iretta Vennay (Veney)	Kilmarnock, VA
Mrs. Robert Wright	Millenbeck, VA
Annie L. Yates	Ottoman, VA

NORTHUMBERLAND COUNTY, VIRGINIA

Mary E. Adams	Avalon, VA
Mollie A. Adams	Avalon, VA
Serih/Sarah Bee	Avalon, VA
Lettie Brown	Lilian, VA
Malindia Buttler	Brown's Store, VA
Julia Campbell	Edwardsville, VA
Sarah Campbell	Lynhams, VA
Polly Carpenter	Remo, VA
Charlotte Davenport	Miskimon, VA
Juddie Dunaway	Rehoboth Church, VA
Malinda Fallin	Lottsburg, VA
Rose Hudnall	Ophelia, VA
Patsy Hughlett	Edwardsville, VA
Nancy Jessup	Remo, VA
Malvina Jones	Heathsville, VA
Eliza Moore	Avalon, VA
Pattie Palmer	Waddy, VA
Mrs. Jane Smith	Ophelia, VA
Mollie Smith	Rehoboth Church, VA
Martha Spence	Brown's Store, VA
Carrie Veney	Lilian, VA
Lillie Veney	Heathsville, VA

Mary Washington   Beverlyville, VA

Jane Wiggins (Mrs.)   Horsehead, VA

Emerline Williams   Sampson's Wharf, VA

RICHMOND COUNTY, VIRGINIA

Matilda Atkins   Ivondale, VA

Claisy/Clarsie Baylor   Warsaw, VA

Anna Bowen   Newland, VA

L. Brown   Village, VA

Martha Burrell   Emmerton, VA

Matilda Churchill   Downings, VA

Mary Ann Clark   Haynesville, VA/Village, VA

Rachel Cox   Havelock, VA

Amie/Amy Hill   Haynesville, VA

Susie Hill   Haynesville, VA

Celia Holmes   Havelock, VA

Cloee Jenkins (Mrs.)   Emmerton, VA

Polly Lewis   Downings, VA

Margaret Lyell   Downings, VA

Henrietta Maiden   Havelock, VA

Isabella Newton   Lyells, VA

Catherine Norris   Downings, VA

Willie Ann Norris   Simonson, VA

Mary J. Owens	Foneswood, VA
Lucy Peterson	Haynesville, VA
Virginia Phillips	Farnham, VA
Henrietta Rich	Sharps Wharf, VA
Sylvia/Sylvie Rich	Emmerton, VA
Airy/Arey/Avery/Eary Shears	Farmer's Fork, VA
Kitty Sorrell	Sharps, VA
Sarah Sydnor	Emmerton, VA
Georgeanna Tate	Lyells, VA
Margaret Thompson	Lyells, VA
Mary Jane Veney	Tidewater, VA
Isabella Williams	Ethel, VA
Virginia Williams	Farnham, VA
Winnie Woodie	Warsaw, VA
Easter Young	Downings, VA

WESTMORELAND COUNTY, VIRGINIA

Sarah Bevely/Beverly (Mrs.)	Maple Grove, VA
Sarah Garner	Oldhams, VA
Cindy Hall	Hinnom, VA
Lizzie Johnson	Templeman, VA
Melinda Richardson	Montross, VA

MIDWIVES WHOSE RESIDENCES WERE NOT ON THE NORTHERN NECK

Sina Davis   Potomac Mills, VA
    (Attended a birth in Westmoreland County, VA.)

Amelia Nash   Granville, VA
    (Attended a birth in Chesterfield County, VA. The baby grew up, moved
    at some point to the Northern Neck of Virginia, and is buried at
    Welcome Grove Baptist Church in Richmond County, VA.)

COUNTY AND STATE REGISTRARS
1900-1919

The following lists contain the names of the local county and state registrars who recorded all births (including home births) in the state of Virginia and more specifically, in Lancaster, Northumberland and Richmond Counties in Virginia. These names were taken from the birth certificates cited in this book.[8]

LANCASTER COUNTY REGISTRARS

E. H. Baker
Miss Jennie Ficklin
L. R. Fleming, JP [Justice of the Peace]
C. Basil Good
P. M. Gresham
Mrs. W. M. Pinckard

NORTHUMBERLAND COUNTY REGISTRARS

Lucille J. Archer
James T. Beane
E. W. Eichelburger
Miss Jennie Ficklin
Margaret Virginia Hinton
Elsa B. Rowe
T. T. Sampson

RICHMOND COUNTY REGISTRARS

Mrs. S. J. Dodson
W. A. Fidler
Susie Headley
Warren Sisson

VIRGINIA STATE REGISTRARS

Arthur W. Clarke (deputy state registrar)
Estelle Marks
Dr. W. A. Plecker
Dorothy J. Winans

---

[8] Source for all images of birth certificates is Ancestry.com, *Virginia, U.S., Birth Records, 1912-2015, Delayed Birth Records, 1721-1920*, accessed 2021-2022.

LANCASTER COUNTY, VIRGINIA, HOME BIRTHS ATTENDED BY DR. C. T. PEIRCE

1900 to 1919

All information and spellings are as they appear on the birth certificates. All birth records are listed in alphabetical order. Race is listed as it appears on the birth certificate.[9]

1. Location of Birth: Co.: Lancaster; District: not given; Town: not given.
    Full Name of Child: Florence Virginia **Alford**.
    Date of Birth: November 2, 1915.
    Father's Name: Henry Timothy Alford, age: 25 yrs., occupation: state roads.
    Race: White.
    Mother's Maiden Name: Florence Etta Hutchings, age: 18 yrs.
    Race: White.
    Delayed Birth Certificate filed with the state registrar on July 17, 1942.

    On the back of this birth certificate, shown below, it states, "Dr Peirce of Nuttsville, Virginia delivered the child named Florence Virginia Alford on Nov 2, 1915." There are also statements attesting to the marriage of the parents on December 2, 1914, at Lancaster Court House by Rev. Combs, and the birth of Shirley Lee Alford on January 15, 1930, in Baltimore, Maryland.

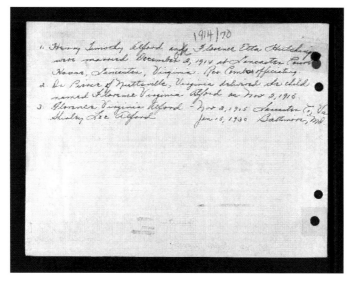

---

[9] Source for all images of birth certificates is Ancestry.com, *Virginia, U.S., Birth Records, 1912-2015, Delayed Birth Records, 1721-1920* [Original data: Virginia, Births, 1721–2015, Virginia Department of Health, Richmond, Virginia], accessed 2021-2022.

2. Location of Birth: Co.: Lancaster; District: White Chapel; Town: Molusk, VA.
    Full Name of Child: Andrew **Ball**.
    Date of Birth: May 22, 1915.
    Father's Name: William Ryland Ball, age: 37, occupation: farmer &
    oysterman.
    Race: Negro.
    Mother's Maiden Name: Lucy Toliaferro, age: 28.
    Race: Negro.
    Original Birth Certificate filed in Lancaster County on June 10, 1915.

3. Location of Birth: Co.: Lancaster; District: White Chapel; Town: Nuttsville.
    Full Name of Child: Cora M. **Ball**.
    Date of Birth: July 31, 1913.
    Father's Name: Warner Ball, age: 38, occupation: day laborer.
    Race: Negro.
    Mother's Maiden Name: Cora Tolliaferro, age: 33.
    Race: Negro.
    Original Birth Certificate filed in Lancaster County on August 4, 1913.

4. Location of Birth: Co.: Lancaster; District: White Chapel; Town: Nuttsville.
    Full Name of Child: Fannie **Ball**.
    Date of Birth: July 10, 1917.
    Father's Name: Warner Ball, age: 42, occupation: day laborer.
    Race: Negro.
    Mother's Maiden Name: Cora Tolliaferro, age: 36.
    Race: Negro.
    Original Birth Record filed in Lancaster County on August 9, 1917.

5. Location of Birth: Co: Lancaster; District: White Chapel; Town: Litwalton.
    Full Name of Child: **Lucile Ball**.
    Date of Birth: September 10, 1919.
    Father's Name: Ryland Ball, age: 40, occupation: farmer.
    Race: Colored.
    Mother's Maiden Name: Lucy Taliaferro, age: 34.
    Race: Colored.
    Original Birth Certificate filed in Lancaster County October 7, 1919.

6. Location of Birth: Co.: Lancaster; District: White Chapel; Town: Ottoman.
    Full Name of Child: Mary Corline **Ball**.
    Date of Birth: September 17, 1919.
    Father's Name: Ford Ball, age: 30, occupation: farmer.
    Race: Negro.
    Mother's Maiden Name: Ida Kelley, age: 29.
    Race: Negro.
    Original Birth Certificate filed in Lancaster County September 25, 1919.

7. Location of Birth: Co.: Lancaster; District: White Chapel; Town: Litwalton.
   Full Name of Child: Paul **Ball**.
   Date of Birth: April 27, 1917.
   Father's Name: W. R. Ball, age: 38, occupation: farmer.
   Race: Negro.
   Mother's Maiden Name: Lucy Tolliaferro, age: 32.
   Race: Negro.
   Original Birth Certificate filed in Lancaster County on May 10, 1917.

8. Location of Birth: Co.: Lancaster; District: White Chapel; Town: Litwalton.
   Full Name of Child: Walter Oneal **Ball**.
   Date of Birth: April 15, 1917.
   Father's Name: Calvin Ball, age: 56, occupation: farmer.
   Race: Negro.
   Mother's Maiden Name: Josephine Jones, age: 34.
   Race: Negro.
   Original Birth Certificate filed in Lancaster County on May 10, 1917.[10]

9. Location of Birth: Co.: Lancaster; District: Mantua; Town: Lively.
   Full Name of Child: Earl Robertson **Barker**.
   Date of Birth: June 3, 1910.
   Father's Name: W. J. Barker, age: 53, occupation: brick mason.
   Race: White.
   Mother's Maiden Name: Mary Lucy Robertson, age: 33.
   Race: White.
   Delayed Birth Certificate filed with the state registrar on June [blank], 1939.

10. Location of Birth: Co.: Lancaster; District: White Chapel; Town: Molusk.
    Full Name of Child: Fleet Everett **Barnes**.
    Date of Birth: December 27, 1916.
    Father's Name: Thomas Barnes, age: 42, occupation: day laborer.
    Race: White.
    Mother's Maiden Name: Jennie Scott, age: 36.
    Race: White.
    Original Birth Certificate filed in Lancaster County on January 10, 1917.

11. Location of Birth: Co.: Lancaster; District: White Chapel; Town: Alfonso.
    Full Name of Child: Clarence Eugene **Barrack** [Jr.].
    Date of Birth: November 16, 1913.
    Father's Name: Clarence Eugene Barrack [Sr.], age: 35, occupation: merchant.
    Race: White.
    Mother's Maiden Name: Bettie Alice Rice, age: 40.
    Race: White.
    Original Birth Certificate filed in Lancaster County on December 9, 1913.

---

[10] See image page vii.

12. Location of Birth: Co.: Lancaster; District: not given; Town: Nuttsville.
Full Name of Child: Edwin Taylor **Barrack**.
Date of Birth: August 11, 1905.
Father's Name: Robert Barrack, age: 58, occupation: farmer.
Race: White.
Mother's Maiden Name: Annie Sanford, age: 31.
Race: White.
Delayed Birth Certificate filed with the state registrar on August 18, 1953.

13. Location of Birth: Co.: Lancaster; District: White Chapel; Town: Litwalton.
Full Name of Child: Alva Floyd **Barton**.
Date of Birth: May 27, 1909.
Father's Name: Julian J. Barton, age: 38, occupation: farmer.
Race: White.
Mother's Maiden Name: Florence Jenette Floyd, age: 25.
Race: White.
Delayed Birth Certificate filed with the state registrar on July 20, 1938.

14. Location of Birth: Co.: Lancaster; District: White Chapel; Town: Litwalton.
Full Name of Child: Julian J. **Barton**, Jr.
Date of Birth: May 10, 1906.
Father's Name: Julian J. Barton [Sr.], age: 35, occupation: farmer.
Race: White.
Mother's Maiden Name: Florence Jenette Floyd, age: 23.
Race: White.
Delayed Birth Certificate filed with the state registrar on July 20, 1938.

15. Location of Birth: Co.: Lancaster; District: White Chapel; Town: Litwalton.
Full Name of Child: Raymond Alexander **Barton**.
Date of Birth: October 13, 1917.
Father's Name: J. J. Barton, age: 49, occupation: farmer.
Race: White.
Mother's Maiden Name: Florence Floyd, age: 34.
Race: White.
Original Birth Certificate filed in Lancaster County on November 10, 1917.

16. Location of Birth: Co.: Lancaster; District: not given; Town: Litwalton.
Full Name of Child: Thomas Albert **Bass**.
Date of Birth: May 27, 1906.
Father's Name: Rosser Lee Bass, age: 39, occupation: not given.
Race: White.
Mother's Maiden Name: Lula Ficklin, age: 34.
Race: White.
Delayed Birth Certificate filed with the state registrar on March 4, 1942.

17. Location of Birth: Co.: Lancaster; District: White Chapel; Town: Molusk.
    Full Name of Child: Elnora **Boyd**.
    Date of Birth: April 26, 1916.
    Father's Name: Nathaniel Boyd, age: 26, occupation: day laborer.
    Race: Negro.
    Mother's Maiden Name: Ada Fauntleroy, age: 23.
    Race: Negro.
    Original Birth Certificate filed in Lancaster County on May 10, 1916.

18. Location of Birth: Co.: Lancaster; District: White Chapel; Town: Molusk.
    Full Name of Child: Selman **Boyd**.
    Date of Birth: September 5, 1917.
    Father's Name: Nathaniel Boyd, age: 37 [possibly age 27], occupation:
    laborer.
    Race: Negro.
    Mother's Maiden Name: Ada Fauntleroy, age: 23.
    Race: Negro.
    Original Birth Certificate filed in Lancaster County on September 10, 1917.

19. Location of Birth: Co.: Lancaster; District: White Chapel; Town: Molusk.
    Full Name of Child: Grace Garnett **Bromley**.
    Date of Birth: January 12, 1918.
    Father's Name: Edward Bromley, age: 52, occupation: day laborer.
    Race: White.
    Mother's Maiden Name: Lilla Anne Saunders, age: 26.
    Race: White.
    Original Birth Certificate filed in Lancaster County on March 11, 1918.[11]

20. Location of Birth: Co.: Lancaster; District: not given; Town: Wheelton.
    Full Name of Child: Annie Street **Brooks**.
    Date of Birth: November 2, 1909.
    Father's Name: Robert Brooks, age: 36, occupation: oyster tonger.
    Race: Negro.
    Mother's Maiden Name: Alice Rich, age: 26.
    Race: Negro.
    Delayed Birth Certificate filed with the state registrar on November 25, 1958.

21. Location of Birth: Co.: Lancaster; District: White Chapel; Town: Molusk.
    Full Name of Child: Extra Dorsey **Brooks**.
    Date of Birth: January 13, 1915.
    Father's Name: Extra Brooks, age: 26, occupation: day laborer.
    Race: Negro.
    Mother's Maiden Name: Neomi Boyd, age: 20.
    Race: Negro.
    Original Birth Certificate filed in Lancaster County on April 1, 1915.

---

[11] There is a second birth certificate for **Grace Garnett Bromley** which is a delayed birth certificate. It gives her birth date as January 12, 1919; father's name as Edward Fitzhugh Bromley (age, occupation, and race the same as above); mother's maiden name as Lillian Ann Sanders, age 28; filed with the state registrar February 18, 1942.

22. Location of Birth: Co.: Lancaster; District: White Chapel; Town: Litwalton.
Full Name of Child: Victoria **Brooks**.
Date of Birth: July 23, 1913.
Father's Name: Robert Brooks, age: 28, occupation: day laborer.
Race: Negro.
Mother's Maiden Name: Alice Rich, age: 23.
Race: Negro.
Original Birth Certificate filed in Lancaster County on July 25, 1913.

23. Location of Birth: Co.: Lancaster; District: White Chapel; Town: Molusk.
Full Name of Child: Armon **Brown**.[12]
Date of Birth: February 27, 1916.
Father's Name: Charles Brown, age: 28, occupation: day laborer.
Race: Negro.
Mother's Maiden Name: Janet Nelms, age: 27.
Race: Negro.
Original Birth Certificate filed in Lancaster County on March 10, 1916.

24. Location of Birth: Co.: Lancaster; District: not given; Town: Litwalton.
Full Name of Child: Charles Monroe **Brown**.
Date of Birth: September 10, 1917.
Father's Name: Wm. H. Brown, age: 45 [probably age 27; he was born in 1890],[13] occupation: Engineer.
Race: White.
Mother's Maiden Name: Addie K. Barrack, age: 43 [probably 25; she was born in 1892].[14]
Race: White.
Delayed Birth Certificate filed with the state registrar on January 17, 1936.

25. Location of Birth: Co.: Lancaster; District: White Chapel; Town: not given.
Full Name of Child: Monnie Helen **Brown**.[15]
Date of Birth: November 8, 1913.
Father's Name: William Henry Brown, age: 21, occupation: farmer.
Race: White.
Mother's Maiden Name: Addie Kate Barrack, age: 21.
Race: White.
Original Birth Certificate filed in Lancaster County on November 15, 1913.

---

[12] At the bottom of the birth certificate, it states, "Given name added from a supplemental report" and it was dated June 5, 1944.
[13] Source: Bethel History Committee, *Bethel Is God's House*, pub. 2011, p. 160.
[14] Source: Bethel History Committee, *Bethel Is God's House*, pub. 2011, p. 160.
[15] At the bottom of the birth certificate, it states, "Name added from attending physician's record and affidavit" and it was dated October 17, 1963.

26. Location of Birth: Co.: Lancaster; District: White Chapel; Town: Molusk.
Full Name of Child: Eddie **Carter**.
Date of Birth: February 28, 1917.
Father's Name: Lumbard Carter, age: 50, occupation: day laborer.
Race: Negro.
Mother's Maiden Name: Maria Ball, age: 40.
Race: Negro.
Original Birth Certificate filed in Lancaster County on March 10, 1917.

27. Location of Birth: Co.: Lancaster; District: White Chapel; Town: Nuttsville.
Full Name of Child: Eugene **Carter** [Jr.].
Date of Birth: September 22, 1913.
Father's Name: Eugene Carter [Sr.], age: 37, occupation: day laborer.
Race: Negro.
Mother's Maiden Name: Alberta Smith, age: 27.
Race: Negro.
Original Birth Certificate filed in Lancaster County on October 8, 1913.

28. Location of Birth: Co.: Lancaster; District: White Chapel; Town: Nuttsville.
Full Name of Child: Geo. [George] Albert **Carter**.
Date of Birth: October 8, 1913.
Father's Name: Lumbard Carter, age: 51, occupation: day laborer.
Race: Negro.
Mother's Maiden Name: Maria Ball, age: 36.
Race: Negro.
Original Birth Certificate filed in Lancaster County on October 15, 1913.

29. Location of Birth: Co.: Lancaster; District: White Chapel; Town: Molusk.
Full Name of Child: Gilbert **Carter**.
Date of Birth: February 2, 1918.
Father's Name: Eugene Carter, age: 40, occupation: farm laborer.
Race: Negro.
Mother's Maiden Name: Alberta Smith, age: 36.
Race: Negro.
Original Birth Certificate filed in Lancaster County on March 11, 1918.

30. Location of Birth: Co.: Lancaster; District: White Chapel; Town: Ottoman.
Full Name of Child: James Henry **Carter**.
Date of Birth: October 7, 1919.
Father's Name: F. P. Carter, age: 21, occupation: farmer.
Race: White.
Mother's Maiden Name: Alice C. Stevens, age: 17.
Race: White.
Original Birth Certificate filed in Lancaster County October 9, 1919.

31. Location of Birth: Co.: Lancaster; District: White Chapel; Town: Nuttsville.
    Full Name of Child: Rufus **Carter**.
    Date of Birth: December 12, 1917.
    Father's Name: Sprig Carter, age: 66, occupation: day laborer.
    Race: Negro.
    Mother's Maiden Name: Alice Boyd, age: 38.
    Race: Negro.
    Original Birth Certificate filed in Lancaster County on January 10, 1918.

32. Location of Birth: Co.: Lancaster; District: White Chapel; Town: Molusk.
    Full Name of Child: Bratton Leroy **Chilton**.
    Date of Birth: March 22, 1916.
    Father's Name: Robert Chilton, age: 23, occupation: fisherman.
    Race: White.
    Mother's Maiden Name: Almira Payne Doggett, age: 23.
    Race: White.
    Original Birth Certificate filed in Lancaster County on April 4, 1916.

33. Location of Birth: Co.: Lancaster; District: not given; Town: Molusk.
    Full Name of Child: Eunice Elizabeth **Chowning**.
    Date of Birth: August 18, 1906.
    Father's Name: Charles Fairfax Chowning, age: 42, occupation: farmer.[16]
    Race: White.
    Mother's Maiden Name: Clara Sarah Barrack, age: 37.
    Race: White.
    Delayed Birth Certificate filed with the state registrar on April 7, 1959.

34. Location of Birth: Co.: Lancaster; District: not given; Town: Molusk.
    Full Name of Child: James Hancock **Chowning**.
    Date of Birth: August 24, 1903.
    Father's Name: Charles Fairfax Chowning, age: 36, occupation: farmer.
    Race: White.
    Mother's Maiden Name: Sarah Clara Barrack Marshall, age: 30.
    Race: White.
    Delayed Birth Certificate filed with the state registrar on September 20, 1958.

35. Location of Birth: Co.: Lancaster; District: Mantua; Town: Lively.
    Full Name of Child: Edward Carlyle Davis **Clark**.
    Date of Birth: October 14, 1916.
    Father's Name: L. R. Clark, age: 49, occupation: carpenter.
    Race: White.
    Mother's Maiden Name: Effus C. Bush, age: 35.
    Race: White.
    Original Birth Certificate filed in Lancaster County on January 9, 1917.

---

[16] At the bottom of the birth certificate, it states, "Marriage record of parents on file in this Bureau show they were married in Lancaster County, in 1902."

36. Location of Birth: Co.: Lancaster; District: Mantua; Town: Lively.
Full Name of Child: Elizabeth Louise **Clark**.
Date of Birth: October 17, 1906.
Father's Name: Clyde B. Clark, age: 33, occupation: mason.
Race: W [White].
Mother's Maiden Name: Elizabeth Euline Revere, age: 29.
Race: W [White].
Delayed Birth Certificate filed with the state registrar on February 14, 1946.

37. Location of Birth: Co.: Lancaster; District: Mantua; Town: Lively.
Full Name of Child: Elsie Graham **Clark**.
Date of Birth: October 10, 1913.
Father's Name: Clarence William Clark, age: 29, occupation: merchant.
Race: White.
Mother's Maiden Name: Christine Carrie Barrack, age: 25.
Race: White.
Original Birth Certificate filed in Lancaster County on October, 1913 [day not given].

38. Location of Birth: Co.: Lancaster; District: Mantua; Town: Lively.
Full Name of Child: Genevieve Pearl **Clark**.
Date of Birth: September 1, 1916.
Father's Name: Clarence Clark, age: 32, occupation: merchant.
Race: White.
Mother's Maiden Name: Cristy Barrack, age: 30.
Race: White.
Original Birth Certificate filed in Lancaster County on January 9, 1917.

39. Location of Birth: Co.: Lancaster; District: not given; Town: not given.
Full Name of Child: Sydnor Bernard **Clark**.
Date of Birth: July 19, 1911.
Father's Name: Lewis Ryland Clark, age: 44, occupation: carpenter.
Race: White.
Mother's Maiden Name: Effus Claybrook Bush, age: 30.
Race: White.
Delayed Birth Certificate filed with the state registrar on July 19, 1955.[17]

40. Location of Birth: Co.: Lancaster; District: White Chapel; Town: not given.
Full Name of Child: Thomas Hodges **Clark**.
Date of Birth: March 15, 1913.
Father's Name: Homer Butts Clark, age: 36, occupation: farmer.
Race: White.
Mother's Maiden Name: Mary Ellen Crockett, age: 40.
Race: White.
Original Birth Certificate filed in Lancaster County on April 18, 1913.

---

[17] At the bottom of this birth certificate, it states, "Dr. C. T. Peirce, the attending physician who signed the certificate above, further certified that the date of this birth was taken from his office records."

41. Location of Birth: Co.: Lancaster; District: Mantua; Town: Miskimon.
Full Name of Child: Clinton Stark **Cockrill**.[18]
Date of Birth: September 6, 1912.
Father's Name: D. W. Cockrill, age: 46, occupation: farmer.
Race: White.
Mother's Maiden Name: Maggie Curren, age: 40.
Race: White.
Original Birth Certificate filed in Lancaster County on September 10, 1912.

42. Location of Birth: Co.: Lancaster; District: White Chapel; Town: Molusk.
Full Name of Child: Adelia **Coleman**.
Date of Birth: September 28, 1919.
Father's Name: Lewis Coleman, age: 47, occupation: day laborer.
Race: Negro.
Mother's Maiden Name: Maggie Thomas, age: 37.
Race: Negro.
Original Birth Certificate filed in Lancaster County September 30, 1919.

43. Location of Birth: Co.: Lancaster; District: White Chapel; Town: Alfonso.
Full Name of Child: Lawrence **Conaway**.
Date of Birth: October 21, 1912.
Father's Name: Louis Conaway, age: 25, occupation: day laborer.
Race: Black.
Mother's Maiden Name: Ivy Fallen, age: 19.
Race: Black.
Original Birth Certificate filed in Lancaster County on October 31, 1912.

44. Location of Birth: Co.: Lancaster; District: White Chapel; Town: Molusk.
Full Name of Child: John **Conrad**.
Date of Birth: February 6, 1915.
Father's Name: Emil Conrad, age: 28, occupation: oyster shucker.
Race: White.
Mother's Maiden Name: Gretchen Korbach, age: 26.
Race: White.
Original Birth Certificate filed in Lancaster County on February 26, 1915.

45. Location of Birth: Co.: Lancaster; District: White Chapel; Town: Molusk.
Full Name of Child: Lottie Stella Peirce **Conrad**.[19]
Date of Birth: August 17, 1918.
Father's Name: Emil Conrad, age: 40 [possibly age 30], occupation: day laborer.
Race: White.
Mother's Maiden Name: Gretchen Korbach, age: 29.
Race: White.
Original Birth Certificate filed in Lancaster County on August 17, 1918.

---

[18] At the bottom of this birth certificate, it states, "Given name added from a supplemental report" and it is dated October 31, 1912.
[19] At the bottom of this birth certificate, it states, "#2 [on the birth certificate line #2] First name added by marriage record and affidavit."

46. Location of Birth: Co.: Lancaster; District: White Chapel; Town: Molusk.
Full Name of Child: Maggie **Conway**.[20]
Date of Birth: November 3, 1916.
Father's Name: Robert Conway, age: 41, occupation: day laborer.
Race: Negro.
Mother's Maiden Name: Julia Ball, age: 36.
Race: Negro.
Original Birth Certificate filed in Lancaster County on November 14, 1916.

47. Location of Birth: Co.: Lancaster; District: White Chapel; Town: Molusk.
Full Name of Child: Milburn James **Corbin**.[21]
Date of Birth: December 30, 1916.
Father's Name: Sam Corbin, age: 27, occupation: oyster shucker.
Race: Negro.
Mother's Maiden Name: N. Kay Bell, age: 14.
Race: Negro.
Original Birth Certificate filed in Lancaster County on January 10, 1917.

48. Location of Birth: Co.: Lancaster; District: White Chapel; Town: Molusk.
Full Name of Child: Thomas Loyd **Croxton**.
Date of Birth: March 14, 1918.
Father's Name: James H. Croxton, age: 41, occupation: day laborer.
Race: Colored.
Mother's Maiden Name: Matilda Laws, age: 37.
Race: Colored.
Original Birth Certificate filed in Lancaster County on April 6, 1918.

49. Location of Birth: Co.: Lancaster; District: Mantua; Town: Alfonso.
Full Name of Child: Luther James **Davenport**.
Date of Birth: June 3, 1915.
Father's Name: Hidie Davenport, age: 28, occupation: day laborer.
Race: Negro.
Mother's Maiden Name: Mattie Wood, age: 25.
Race: Negro.
Original Birth Certificate filed in Lancaster County on June 14, 1915.

50. Location of Birth: Co.: Lancaster; District: White Chapel; Town: Molusk.
Full Name of Child: Eddie **Dawson**.
Date of Birth: June 18, 1919.
Father's Name: Columbus Dawson, age: 36, occupation: day laborer.
Race: White.
Mother's Maiden Name: Bessie Enos, age: 47.
Race: White.
Original Birth Certificate filed in Lancaster County July 14, 1919.

---

[20] At the bottom of this birth certificate, it states, "Given name added & spelling of surname corrected by affidavit & social security record." It is dated May 26, 1976.
[21] The surname of this child (Corbin) is marked out on the birth certificate and the name "Bell" is written above it.

51. Location of Birth: Co.: Lancaster; District: White Chapel; Town: Litwalton.
    Full Name of Child: Howard Elmore **Dawson**.[22]
    Date of Birth: September 10, 1912.
    Father's Name: S. W. Dawson, age: 57, occupation: farmer.
    Race: White.
    Mother's Maiden Name: Emma Elmore, age: 30.
    Race: White.
    Original Birth Certificate filed in Lancaster County on September 13, 1912.

52. Location of Birth: Co.: Lancaster; District: White Chapel; Town: Litwalton.
    Full Name of Child: William Baten **Dawson** [Jr.].
    Date of Birth: February 18, 1913.
    Father's Name: William Baten Dawson [Sr.], age: 30, occupation: farmer.
    Race: White.
    Mother's Maiden Name: Laura Jenette Brown, age: 26.
    Race: White.
    Original Birth Certificate filed in Lancaster County on March 15, 1913.

53. Location of Birth: Co.: Lancaster; District: White Chapel; Town: Litwalton.
    Full Name of Child: Lewis Elmore **Dodson**.
    Date of Birth: August 2, 1913.
    Father's Name: Gilliam Bates Dodson, age: 33, occupation: merchant.
    Race: White.
    Mother's Maiden Name: Kate Lauren Elmore, age: 34.
    Race: White.
    Original Birth Certificate filed in Lancaster County on August 6, 1913.

54. Location of Birth: Co.: Lancaster; District: White Chapel; Town: Molusk.
    Full Name of Child: Arthur Howard **Doggett**.
    Date of Birth: June 12, 1919.
    Father's Name: Cleveland Doggett, age: 35, occupation: clerk.
    Race: White.
    Mother's Maiden Name: Corry Taft, age: 31.
    Race: White.
    Original Birth Certificate filed in Lancaster County July 14, 1919.

55. Location of Birth: Co.: Lancaster; District: White Chapel; Town: Nuttsville.
    Full Name of Child: Mary Elizabeth **Doggett**.
    Date of Birth: July 17, 1913.
    Father's Name: Cleveland Doggett, age: 29, occupation: clerk in store.
    Race: White.
    Mother's Maiden Name: Mollie Anne Taff [Taft], age: 25.
    Race: White.
    Original Birth Certificate filed in Lancaster County on July 25, 1913.[23]

---

[22] At the bottom of this birth certificate, it states, "Given name added from a certificate on back signed by mother." It is dated October 29, 1912.

[23] See image on page vi.

56. Location of Birth: Co.: Lancaster; District: not given; Town: not given.
    Full Name of Child: Helen Louise **Douglas**.
    Date of Birth: June 18, 1909.[24]
    Father's Name: Edwin James Douglas, age: 30, occupation: farmer.
    Race: White.
    Mother's Maiden Name: Fannie Louise Barnes, age: 29.
    Race: White.
    Delayed Birth Certificate filed with the state registrar on April 11, 1955.

57. Location of Birth: Co.: Lancaster; District: not given; Town: Mollusk.
    Full Name of Child: Marian Almeria **Douglas**.
    Date of Birth: September 7, 1905.[25]
    Father's Name: Edward Jennings Douglas, age: 28, occupation: mfg. of lumber.
    Race: White.
    Mother's Maiden Name: Fannie Louise Barnes, age: 27.
    Race: White.
    Delayed Birth Certificate filed with the state registrar on October 19, 1955.

58. Location of Birth: Co.: Lancaster; District: Mantua; Town: Lively.
    Full Name of Child: Mildred Lee **Dudley**.
    Date of Birth: July 17, 1917.
    Father's Name: Adolphus Dudley, age: 29, occupation: farmer.
    Race: White.
    Mother's Maiden Name: Misoura Smith, age: 23.
    Race: White.
    Original Birth Certificate filed in Lancaster County on January 11, 1918.

59. Location of Birth: Co.: Lancaster; District: White Chapel; Town: Ottoman.
    Full Name of Child: Howard Elliott **Dunaway**.
    Date of Birth: June 19, 1917.
    Father's Name: Hiram E. Dunaway, age: 27, occupation: merchant.
    Race: White.
    Mother's Maiden Name: Ruth B. Haynie, age: 23.
    Race: White.
    Original Birth Certificate filed in Lancaster County on August 10, 1917.

---

[24] At the bottom of this birth certificate, it states, "Dr. C. T. Peirce states that the date of birth of Helen Louise Douglas, June 18, 1909, was taken from his private records." A second statement on this document states, "Record of parents' marriage shows Edwin Douglas born in Richmond, Co., VA, and Fannie Barnes born in Lancaster Co., VA."

[25] At the bottom of this birth certificate, it states, "Dr. C. T. Peirce, M. D., states that the birthdate of Marian Almeria Douglas came from his private records."

60. Location of Birth: Co.: Lancaster; District: not given; Town: Litwalton.
Full Name of Child: Cora Dallas **Elmore**.
Date of Birth: October 7, 1909.
Father's Name: C. R. Elmore, age: 27, occupation: not given.
Race: White.
Mother's Maiden Name: Mary Virginia Elmore, age: 22.
Race: White.
Delayed Birth Certificate filed with the state registrar on September 9, 1946.

61. Location of Birth: Co.: Lancaster; District: White Chapel; Town: Litwalton.
Full Name of Child: Marvin Randolph **Elmore**.
Date of Birth: January 16, 1907.
Father's Name: C. R. Elmore, age: 24, occupation: marine ( ) [unreadable].
Race: White.
Mother's Maiden Name: Mary Virginia Elmore, age: 20.
Race: White.
Delayed Birth Certificate filed with the state registrar on July 29, 1939.

62. Location of Birth: Co.: Lancaster; District: White Chapel; Town: Molusk.
Full Name of Child: Alberta **Fallin**.
Date of Birth: October 30, 1916.
Father's Name: Theodore Fallin, age: 42, occupation: day laborer.
Race: Negro.
Mother's Maiden Name: Sarah Kelley, age: 39.
Race: Negro.
Original Birth Certificate filed in Lancaster County on November 14, 1916.

63. Location of Birth: Co.: Lancaster; District: White Chapel; Town: Nuttsville.
Full Name of Child: Sarah **Fallin**.
Date of Birth: August 5, 1912.
Father's Name: Theodore Fallin, age: 36, occupation: farmer & oysterman.
Race: Negro.
Mother's Maiden Name: Sarah Kelley, age: 37.
Race: Negro.
Original Birth Certificate filed in Lancaster County on August 31, 1912.

64. Location of Birth: Co.: Lancaster; District: White Chapel; Town: Molusk.
Full Name of Child: Robert Kelley **Fauntleroy**.
Date of Birth: August 6, 1916.
Father's Name: Unknown [Nothing was known about this father].
Mother's Maiden Name: Ra Fauntleroy, age: 22.
Race: Negro.
Original Birth Certificate filed in Lancaster County on August 12, 1916.

65. Location of Birth: Co.: Lancaster; District: White Chapel; Town: Litwalton.
Full Name of Child: Albert **Fisher**.
Date of Birth: March 17, 1913.
Father's Name: Edward Fisher, age: 35, occupation: day laborer.
Race: White.
Mother's Maiden Name: Lucille Elmore, age: 25.
Race: White.
Original Birth Certificate filed in Lancaster County on April 18, 1913.

66. Location of Birth: Co.: Lancaster; District: White Chapel; Town: Molusk.
Full Name of Child: Francis Elmore **Fisher**.
Date of Birth: April 3, 1916.
Father's Name: Edward Fisher, age: 38, occupation: day laborer.
Race: White.
Mother's Maiden Name: Lucile Elmore, age: 27.
Race: White.
Original Birth Certificate filed in Lancaster County on May 10, 1916.

At the bottom of this birth certificate, in an entry dated December 15, 1943, it states, "Given name added from a supplemental report...from a list of children." The list of the nine Fisher children, shown below, is filed with the birth certificate.

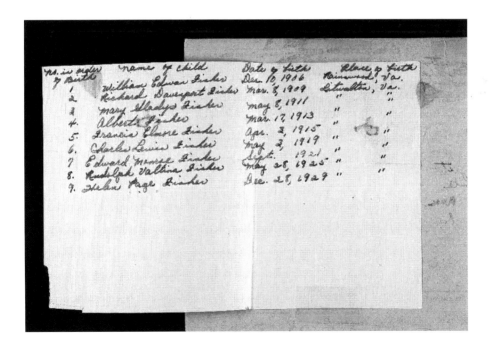

67. Location of Birth: Co.: Lancaster; District: White Chapel; Town: Molusk.
Full Name of Child: John Raymond Napoleon **Gaskins**.
Date of Birth: April 20, 1919.
Father's Name: John Gaskins, age: 24, occupation: Private US Navy France.
Race: Colored.
Mother's Maiden Name: Priscilla Coleman, age: 20.
Race: Colored.
Original Birth Certificate filed in Lancaster County April 24, 1919.

68. Location of Birth: Co.: Lancaster; District: White Chapel; Town: Molusk.
Full Name of Child: Elmer **Gray**.
Date of Birth: January 29, 1917.
Father's Name: Robert Gray, age: 40, occupation: day laborer.
Race: Colored.
Mother's Maiden Name: Mary Gordon, age: 28.
Race: Colored.
Original Birth Certificate filed in Lancaster County on February 9, 1917.

69. Location of Birth: Co.: Lancaster; District: White Chapel; Town: Molusk.
Full Name of Child: Laura Virginia **Gray**. [One of a set of twins; see record 70.]
Date of Birth: December 27, 1915.
Father's Name: Benjamin J. Gray, age: 46, occupation: oyster shucker.
Race: Colored.
Mother's Maiden Name: Priscillia Rich, age: 28.
Race: Colored.
Original Birth Certificate filed in Lancaster County on January 31, 16.

70. Location of Birth: Co.: Lancaster; District: White Chapel; Town: Molusk.
Full Name of Child: Sarah Fannie **Gray**. [One of a set of twins; see record 69.]
Date of Birth: December 27, 1915.
Father's Name: Benjamin J. Gray, age: 46, occupation: oyster shucker.
Race: Colored.
Mother's Maiden Name: Priscillia Rich, age: 28.
Original Birth Certificate filed in Lancaster County on January 31, 1916.

71. Location of Birth: Co.: Lancaster; District: White Chapel; Town: Molusk.
Full Name of Child: Ruth **Gray** [Grey on birth certificate].
Date of Birth: August 21, 1917.
Father's Name: Ben Gray, age: 50, occupation: day laborer.
Race: Negro.
Mother's Maiden Name: Priscilla Rich, age: 38 [possibly age 30].
Race: Negro.
Original Birth Certificate filed in Lancaster County on September 10, 1917.

72. Location of Birth: Co.: Lancaster; District: not given; Town: Ottoman.
    Full Name of Child: Frances Chilton **Gresham**.
    Date of Birth: July 13, 1907.
    Father's Name: George Sanford Gresham, age: 26, occupation: salesman.
    Race: White.
    Mother's Maiden Name: Fannie Jones Chilton, age: 26.
    Race: White.
    Delayed Birth Certificate filed with the state registrar on September 14, 1951.

73. Location of Birth: Co.: Lancaster; District: White Chapel; Town: Molusk.
    Full Name of Child: Morris Lewis **Grey**.
    Date of Birth: February 21, 1915.
    Father's Name: Robert Grey, age: 35, occupation: day laborer.
    Race: Negro.
    Mother's Maiden Name: Mary Gordon, age: 22.
    Race: Negro.
    Original Birth Certificate filed in Lancaster County on March 1, 1915.

74. Location of Birth: Co.: Lancaster; District: White Chapel; Town: Senora.
    Full Name of Child: Gladys Gertrude **Haislip**.
    Date of Birth: June 9, 1919.
    Father's Name: Julian Haislip, age: 25, occupation: day laborer.
    Race: White.
    Mother's Maiden Name: Annie Dodson, age: 23.
    Race: White.
    Original Birth Certificate filed in Lancaster County June 21, 1919.

75. Location of Birth: County: Lancaster; District: White Chapel; Town: not given.
    Full Name of Child: Elias **Harris**. [One of a set of twins; see record 77.]
    Date of Birth: April 23, 1917.
    Father's Name: Elias Harris, age: 40, occupation: day laborer.
    Race: Negro.
    Mother's Maiden Name: Lillie Boyd, age: 30.
    Race: Negro.
    Original Birth Certificate filed in Lancaster County on May 10, 1917.

76. Location of Birth: Co.: Lancaster; District: White Chapel; Town: Molusk.
    Full Name of Child: Elizabeth **Harris**.
    Date of Birth: April 6, 1919.
    Father's Name: William Harris, age: 45, occupation: day laborer.
    Race: Negro.
    Mother's Maiden Name: Mary Fallin, age: 24.
    Race: Negro.
    Original Birth Certificate filed in Lancaster County April 12, 1919.

77. Location of Birth: Co.: Lancaster; District: White Chapel; Town: not given.
    Full Name of Child: Lillie A. **Harris**. [One of a set of twins; see record 75.]
    Date of Birth: April 23, 1917.
    Father's Name: Elias Harris, age: 40, occupation: day laborer.
    Race: Negro.
    Mother's Maiden Name: Lillie Boyd, age: 30.
    Race: Negro.
    Original Birth Certificate filed in Lancaster County on May 10, 1917.

78. Location of Birth: Co.: Lancaster; District: White Chapel; Town: Molusk.
    Full Name of Child: William Robert **Harris**.
    Date of Birth: August 15, 1916.
    Father's Name: William Harris, age: 41, occupation: day laborer.
    Race: Negro.
    Mother's Maiden Name: Mary Lizzie Fallin, age: 20.
    Race: Negro.
    Original Birth Certificate filed in Lancaster County on September 11, 1916.

79. Location of Birth: Co.: Lancaster; District: Mantua; Town: Alfonso.
    Full Name of Child: Addie Pleasant **Haynie**.[26]
    Date of Birth: August 2, 1913.
    Father's Name: Morgan Haynie, age: 39, Occupation: blacksmith.
    Race: White.
    Mother's Maiden Name: Sadie Viola Marsh, age: 36.
    Race: White.
    Original Birth Certificate filed in Lancaster County on August 11, 1913.

80. Location of Birth: Co.: Lancaster; District: White Chapel; Town: Molusk.
    Full Name of Child: Altrace Virginia **Haynie**.
    Date of Birth: August 2, 1917.
    Father's Name: E. W. Haynie, age: 35, occupation: day laborer.
    Race: White.
    Mother's Maiden Name: Gladys Saunders, age: 18.
    Race: White.
    Original Birth Certificate filed in Lancaster County on August 9, 1917.

81. Location of Birth: Co.: Lancaster; District: Mantua; Town: Alfonso.
    Full Name of Child: Eloise Tapscott **Haynie**.
    Date of Birth: October 23, 1911.
    Father's Name: W. W. Haynie, age: 38, occupation: carpenter.
    Race: W [White].
    Mother's Maiden Name: Ella Leona Walker, age: 33.
    Race: W [White].
    Delayed Birth Certificate filed with the state registrar on October 8, 1948.[27]

---

[26] At the bottom of this birth certificate, it states, "Given name added from a supplemental report, Mother." It is dated September 18, 1939.

[27] A second filing date was given for this birth as August 17, 1948 with the local (Lancaster County) registrar.

82. Location of Birth: Co.: Lancaster; District: not given; Town: Lively.
Full Name of Child: Ernest Ward **Haynie**.
Date of Birth: August 6, 1911.
Father's Name: E. H. Haynie, age: 32, occupation: farmer.
Race: W [White].
Mother's Maiden Name: Mary Geneva Dudley, age: 30.
Race: W [White].
Delayed Birth Certificate filed with the state registrar on September 25, 1941.

83. Location of Birth: Co.: Lancaster; District: Mantua; Town: Alfonso.
Full Name of Child: Florence Virginia **Haynie**.
Date of Birth: July 16, 1915.
Father's Name: William E. Haynie, age: 41, occupation: farmer.
Race: White.
Mother's Maiden Name: Ella Walker, age: 36.
Race: White.
Original Birth Certificate filed in Lancaster County on June 16, 1917.[28]

84. Location of Birth: Co.: Lancaster; District: Mantua; Town: Alfonso.
Full Name of Child: Gwendolyn Albaugh **Haynie**.
Date of Birth: January 8, 1908.
Father's Name: W. W. **Haynie**, age: 34, occupation: carpenter.
Race: W [White].
Mother's Maiden Name: Ella Leona Walker, age: 29.
Race: W [White].
Delayed Birth Certificate filed with the state registrar October 8, 1948.[29]

85. Location of Birth: Co.: Lancaster; District: White Chapel; Town: Lively.
Full Name of Child: Homer C. **Haynie**, Jr.
Date of Birth: October 6, 1919.
Father's Name: Homer C. Haynie [Sr.], age: 30, occupation: farmer.
Race: White.
Mother's Maiden Name: Hester Olliver, age: 26.
Race: White.
Original Birth Certificate filed in Lancaster County October 20, 1919.

86. Location of Birth: Co.: Lancaster: District: Mantua; Town: Alfonso.
Full Name of Child: Joseph Gordon **Haynie**.
Date of Birth: January 7, 1918.
Father's Name: W. E. Haynie, age: 43, occupation: farmer.
Race: White.
Mother's Maiden Name: Ella Walker, age: 38.
Race: White.
Original Birth Certificate filed in Lancaster County on January 11, 1918.

---

[28] This could almost be classified as a Delayed Birth Certificate since nearly two years went by before it was filed.

[29] A second filing date was given for this birth as August 17, 1948 with the local registrar.

87. Location of Birth: Co.: Lancaster; District: Mantua; Town: Alfonso.
    Full Name of Child: Littleton Harmon **Haynie.**
    Date of Birth: January 20, 1906.
    Father's Name: W. E. Haynie, age: 32, occupation: carpenter.
    Race: White.
    Mother's Maiden Name: Ella Lena Walker, age: 27.
    Race: White.
    Delayed Birth Certificate filed with the state registrar on March 2, 1941.

88. Location of Birth: Co.: Lancaster; District: White Chapel; Town: Alfonso.
    Full Name of Child: Llewellyn Ford **Haynie.**[30]
    Date of Birth: April 8, 1919.
    Father's Name: J. Morgan Haynie, age: 44, occupation: merchant.
    Race: White.
    Mother's Maiden Name: Sadie V. Marsh, age: 42.
    Race: White.
    Original Birth Certificate filed in Lancaster County April 12, 1919.

89. Location of Birth: Co.: Lancaster; District: not given; Town: not given.
    Full Name of Child: Nellie Katherine **Haynie**.
    Date of Birth: January 2, 1907.
    Father's Name: Edwin Franklin Haynie, age: 36, occupation: not given.
    Race: White.
    Mother's Maiden Name: Mary Lelia Cox, age: 29.
    Race: White.
    Delayed Birth Certificate filed with the state registrar on August 6, 1942.

90. Location of Birth: Co.: Lancaster; District: Mantua; Town: Alfonso.
    Full Name of Child: Robert Eugene **Haynie**.
    Date of Birth: July 18, 1913.
    Father's Name: William E. Haynie, age: 39, occupation: farmer.
    Race: White.
    Mother's Maiden Name: Ella L. Walker, age: 34.
    Race: White.
    Original Birth Certificate filed in Lancaster County on August 16, 1913.

91. Location of Birth: Co.: Lancaster; District: not given; Town: Alfonso.
    Full Name of Child: Wakelin Woodroe **Haynie**. [31]
    Date of Birth: November 30, 1916.
    Father's Name: J. M. Haynie, age: 42, occupation: merchant.
    Race: White.
    Mother's Maiden Name: Sadie Marsh, age: 40.
    Race: White.
    Original Birth Certificate filed in Lancaster County on January 9, 1917.

---

[30] At the bottom of this birth certificate, it states, "Given name added from a supplemental report." It is dated August 7, 1919 and signed by state registrar W. A. Plecker, M. D.

[31] At the bottom of this birth certificate, it states, "Given name added from a supplemental report." It is dated May 3, 1917.

92. Location of Birth: Co.: Lancaster; District: not given; Town: Alfonso.
    Full Name of Child: William Walker **Haynie**.
    Date of Birth: September 23, 1909.
    Father's Name: William Eugene Haynie, age: 36, occupation: farmer.
    Race: White.
    Mother's Maiden Name: Ella Lena Walker, age: 31.
    Race: White.
    Delayed Birth Certificate filed with the state registrar on February 19, 1941.

93. Location of Birth: Co.: Lancaster; District: White Chapel; Town: Molusk.
    Full Name of Child: Thomas William **Hayward**.
    Date of Birth: March 11, 1918.
    Father's Name: Richard Hayward, age: 50, occupation: day laborer.
    Race: White.
    Mother's Maiden Name: Fannie Bush, age: 34.
    Race: White.
    Original Birth Certificate filed in Lancaster County on April 18, 1918.

94. Location of Birth: Co.: Lancaster; District: White Chapel; Town: Ottoman.
    Full Name of Child: Elsie Virginia **Hazzard**.
    Date of Birth: March 1, 1919.
    Father's Name: C. G. Hazzard, age: 38, occupation: day laborer.
    Race: White.
    Mother's Maiden Name: E. Virginia Bartlett, age: 39.
    Race: White.
    Original Birth Certificate filed in Lancaster County March 8, 1919.

95. Location of Birth: Co.: Lancaster; District: White Chapel; Town: Ottoman.
    Full Name of Child: Ruth Annett **Hazzard**.
    Date of Birth: December 14, 1917.
    Father's Name: Chester Garfield Hazzard, age: 36, occupation: driver on public road construction.
    Race: White American.
    Mother's Maiden Name: Eliza Virginia Bartlett, age: 37.
    Race: White American.
    Original Birth Certificate filed in Lancaster County on January 26, 1918.

96. Location of Birth: Co.: Lancaster; District: not given; Town: Miskimon.[32]
    Full Name of Child: Joseph Peirce **Headley**.
    Date of Birth: April 28, 1908.
    Father's Name: Kenner Lloyd Headley, age: 29, occupation: keeping a country store.
    Race: White American.
    Mother's Maiden Name: Ethel Augustus Pittman, age: 22.
    Race: White American.
    Delayed Birth Certificate filed with the state registrar on July 1, 1941.

---

[32] At the time of this printing, the town of Miskimon is in Northumberland County, VA on the county line with Lancaster County.

97. Location of Birth: Co.: Lancaster; District: Mantua; Town: Lively.
Full Name of Child: Leslie Peirce **Hinton**.
Date of Birth: October 25, 1917.
Father's Name: N. R. Hinton, age: 30, occupation: farmer.
Race: White.
Mother's Maiden Name: Edna Beane, age: 28.
Race: White.
Original Birth Certificate filed in Lancaster County on January 11, 1918.

98. Location of Birth: Co.: Lancaster; District: White Chapel; Town: Morattico.
Full Name of Child: Ethel Alces **Howeth**.
Date of Birth: October 11, 1911.
Father's Name: G. O. Howeth, age: 42, occupation: oyster packer.
Race: White.
Mother's Maiden Name: Lillie Irene Towles, age: 33.
Race: White.
Delayed Birth Certificate filed with local registrar on November 7, 1939.

99. Location of Birth: Co.: Lancaster; District: White Chapel; Town: Molusk.
Full Name of Child: Fannie Virginia **Hutchings**.
Date of Birth: February 12, 1916.
Father's Name: Walter W. Hutchings, age: 52, occupation: farmer.
Race: White.
Mother's Maiden Name: Bessie Johnson, age: 32.
Race: White.
Original Birth Certificate filed in Lancaster County on March 10, 1916.

100. Location of Birth: Co.: Lancaster; District: White Chapel; Town: Molusk.
Full Name of Child: Edward **Jurdon**.
Date of Birth: October 27, 1919.
Father's Name: Richard Jurdon, age: 25, occupation: oysterman.
Race: Colored.
Mother's Maiden Name: Rosa Carter, age: 28.
Race: Colored.
Original Birth Certificate filed in Lancaster County January 9, 1920.

101. Location of Birth: Co.: Lancaster; District: White Chapel; Town: Molusk.
Full Name of Child: Hilda Anna **Jurdon**.
Date of Birth: May 29, 1917.
Father's Name: Richard Jurdon, age: 25, occupation: farmer.
Race: Negro.
Mother's Maiden Name: Rosa Carter; age: 27.
Race: Negro.
Original Birth Certificate filed in Lancaster County on June 9, 1917.

102. Location of Birth: Co.: Lancaster; District: White Chapel; Town: Molusk.
Full Name of Child: Richard Edwin **Jurdon**.
Date of Birth: January 7, 1915.
Father's Name: Richard Jurdon, age: 23, occupation: day laborer.
Race: Negro.
Mother's Maiden Name: Rosa Carter, age: 23.
Race: Negro.
Original Birth Certificate filed in Lancaster County on May 1, 1915.

103. Location of Birth: Co.: Lancaster; District: White Chapel; Town: Molusk.
Full Name of Child: Hensley **Kelley**.
Date of Birth: July 15, 1917.
Father's Name: Roger Kelley, age: 38, occupation: day laborer.
Race: Negro.
Mother's Maiden Name: Sarah Griffin, age: 30.
Race: Negro.
Original Birth Certificate filed in Lancaster County on August 9, 1917.

104. Location of Birth: Co.: Lancaster; District: White Chapel; Town: Molusk.
Full Name of Child: Gordon Chin Tapscott **Kirkham**.
Date of Birth: July 6, 1919.
Father's Name: George Otis Kirkham, age: 47, occupation: road constructor.
Race: White.
Mother's Maiden Name: Minnie E. Ketner, age: 35.
Race: White.
Original Birth Certificate filed in Lancaster County July 14, 1919.

105. Location of Birth: Co.: Lancaster; District: White Chapel; Town: Morattico.
Full Name of Child: Walter Addison **Lankford.**
Date of Birth: March 7, 1911.
Father's Name: F. G. Lankford, age: 42, occupation: salesman.
Race: W [White].
Mother's Maiden Name: Alma Coulbourn, age: 34.
Race: W [White].
Delayed Birth Certificate filed with the state registrar on February 18, 1941.

106. Location of Birth: Co.: Lancaster; District: White Chapel; Town: Litwalton.
Full Name of Child: Helen **Laws**.
Date of Birth: July 29, 1913.
Father's Name: Hiram Laws, age: 35, occupation: day laborer.
Race: Negro.
Mother's Maiden Name: Harriot Brooks, age: 21.
Race: Negro.
Original Birth Certificate filed in Lancaster County on August 2, 1913.

107. Location of Birth: Co.: Lancaster; District: White Chapel; Town: Molusk.
Full Name of Child: Josephine Elizabeth **Lee**.
Date of Birth: June 28, 1917.
Father's Name: Cornelius Lee, age: 32, occupation: day laborer.
Race: Negro.
Mother's Maiden Name: Julia Anne Henderson, age: 24.
Race: Negro.
Original Birth Certificate filed in Lancaster County on September 10, 1917.

108. Location of Birth: Co.: Lancaster; District: White Chapel; Town: Molusk.
Full Name of Child: Lottie **Lee**.
Date of Birth: May 28, 1916.
Father's Name: John Lee, age: 22, occupation: day laborer.
Race: Negro.
Mother's Maiden Name: Josephine Henderson, age: 20.
Race: Negro.
Original Birth Certificate filed in Lancaster County on June 8, 1916.[33]

109. Location of Birth: Co.: Lancaster; District: White Chapel; Town: Boer.
Full Name of Child: Louise **Lee.**
Date of Birth: November 7, 1913.
Father's Name: Noble Lee, age: 23, occupation: day laborer.
Race: Negro.
Mother's Maiden Name: Bessie Carter, age: 22.
Race: Negro.
Original Birth Certificate filed in Lancaster County on December 9, 1913.

110. Location of Birth: Co.: Lancaster; District: White Chapel; Town: Boer.
Full Name of Child: Raymond **Lee**.
Date of Birth: October 8, 1917.
Father's Name: Noble Lee, age: 33, occupation: day laborer.
Race: Negro.
Mother's Maiden Name: Bessie [probably Carter] Lee, age: 27.
Race: Negro.
Original Birth Certificate filed in Lancaster County on November 10, 1917.

111. Location of Birth: Co.: Lancaster; District: White Chapel; Town: Nuttsville.
Full Name of Child: Elizabeth **Lewis**.
Date of Birth: July 27, 1919.
Father's Name: Hiram Lewis, age: 40, occupation: day laborer.
Race: Negro.
Mother's Maiden Name: Harriet Brooks, age: 26.
Race: Negro.
Original Birth Certificate filed in Lancaster County October 7, 1919.

---

[33] The child's name (Lottie Lee) was not on the original birth certificate. There is a note at the bottom of the certificate which states, "Name added by marriage record on July 9, 1979" and the birth certificate was called an Amended Birth Certificate.

112. Location of Birth: Lancaster; District: White Chapel; Town: Lively.
Full Name of Child: Evlin Grey **Lewis**.
Date of Birth: August 28, 1913.
Father's Name: Julian Monroe Lewis, age: 30, occupation: engineer.
Race: White.
Mother's Maiden Name: Addie Mertine Jones, age: 32.
Race: White.
Original Birth Certificate filed in Lancaster County on September 11, 1913.

113. Location of Birth: Co.: Lancaster; District: Mantua; Town: Lively.
Full Name of Child: Garland Monroe **Lewis**.
Date of Birth: December 8, 1919.
Father's Name: Monroe Lewis, age: 37, occupation: lumber manufacturer.
Race: White.
Mother's Maiden Name: Addie Jones, age: 38.
Race: White.
Original Birth Certificate filed in Lancaster County September 7, 1920.

114. Location of Birth: Co.: Lancaster; District: Mantua; Town: Lively.
Full Name of Child: Meredith **Lewis**.
Date of Birth: May 17, 1916.
Father's Name: Monroe Lewis, age: 34, occupation: day laborer.
Race: White.
Mother's Maiden Name: Addie Jones, age: 36.
Race: White.
Original Birth Certificate filed in Lancaster County on January 9, 1917.

115. Location of Birth: Co.: Lancaster; District: not given; Town: Lively.
Full Name of Child: Tennyson William Thelbert **Lewis**.
Date of Birth: December 28, 1911.
Father's Name: Thelbert Theodore Lewis, age: 45, occupation: blacksmith.
Race: White.
Mother's Maiden Name: Hettie Annie Marsh, age: 31.
Race: White.
Delayed Birth Certificate filed with the state registrar on September 2, 1941.

116. Location of Birth: Co.: Lancaster; District: White Chapel; Town: Litwalton.
Full Name of Child: Thomas K. **Lewis**.
Date of Birth: December 23, 1917.
Father's Name: T. K. Lewis, age: 29, occupation: clerk.
Race: White.
Mother's Maiden Name: Avelon Adams, age: 26.
Race: White.
Original Birth Certificate filed in Lancaster County on January 10, 1918.

117. Location of Birth: Co.: Lancaster; District: Mantua; Town: Lively.
Full Name of Child: Velma Lee **Lewis**.
Date of Birth: May 6, 1915.
Father's Name: Monroe Lewis, age: 32, occupation: day laborer.
Race: White.
Mother's Maiden Name: Addie Jones, age: 34.
Race: White.
Original Birth Certificate filed in Lancaster County on June 14, 1915.

118. Location of Birth: Co.: Lancaster; District: White Chapel; Town: Molusk.
Full Name of Child: Grace Evelyn **Lusby**.
Date of Birth: February 6, 1916.
Father's Name: Charles Irvin Lusby, age: 27, occupation: farmer.
Race: White.
Mother's Maiden Name: Grace Anne Doggett, age: 25.
Race: White.
Original Birth Certificate filed in Lancaster County on March 10, 1916.

119. Location of Birth: Co.: Lancaster; District: White Chapel; Town: Molusk.
Full Name of Child: Virginia Elaine **Lusby**.
Date of Birth: May 23, 1917.
Father's Name: Irvin Lusby, age: 29, occupation: day laborer.
Race: White.
Mother's Maiden Name: Grace Doggett, age: 27.
Race: White.
Original Birth Certificate filed in Lancaster County on June 16, 1917.

120. Location of Birth: Co.: Lancaster; District: Mantua; Town: Lively.
Full Name of Child: Hugh Peirce **Marsh**.
Date of Birth: December 27, 1917.
Father's Name: John Marsh, age: 33, occupation: farmer.
Race: White.
Mother's Maiden Name: Nora Virginia Revere, age: 32.
Race: White.
Original Birth Certificate filed in Lancaster County on January 11, 1918.

121. Location of Birth: Co.: Lancaster; District: Mantua; Town: Miskimon.[34]
Full Name of Child: Lawrence T. **Marsh**, Jr.
Date of Birth: June 12, 1918.
Father's Name: Lawrence T. Marsh [Sr.], age: 22, occupation: farmer.
Race: White.
Mother's Maiden Name: Ila B. Boothe, age: 17.
Race: White.
Original Birth Certificate filed in Lancaster County on August 31, 1918.

---

[34] At the time of this printing, the town of Miskimon is in Northumberland County, VA on the county line with Lancaster County.

122. Location of Birth: Co.: Lancaster; District: Mantua; Town: Lively.
Full Name of Child: Walter Revere **Marsh**.
Date of Birth: May 17, 1915.
Father's Name: John C. Marsh, age: 30, occupation: farmer.
Race: White.
Mother's Maiden Name: Virginia Revere, age: 30.
Race: White.
Original Birth Certificate filed in Lancaster County on June 14, 1915.

123. Location of Birth: Co.: Lancaster; District: White Chapel; Town: Molusk.
Full Name of Child: James Campbell **McCarty**.
Date of Birth: March 16, 1904.
Father's Name: B. F. McCarty, age: 50, occupation: farmer.
Race: White.
Mother's Maiden Name: Louisa Anna Bland Spencer, age: 33.
Race: White.
Delayed Birth Certificate filed with the state registrar on September 17, 1940.

124. Location of Birth: Co.: Lancaster; District: White Chapel; Town: Molusk.
Full Name of Child: Ovid Roy **McCarty**.
Date of Birth: October 21, 1906.
Father's Name: B. F. McCarty, age: 52, occupation: farmer.
Race: White.
Mother's Maiden Name: Louisa Anna Bland Spencer, age: 35.
Race: White.
Delayed Birth Certificate filed with the state registrar on September 17, 1940.

125. Location of Birth: Co.: Lancaster; District: White Chapel; Town: Molusk.
Full Name of Child: Charles Fred **Miles**.[35]
Date of Birth: March 13, 1918.
Father's Name: James Miles, age: 43, occupation: farmer.
Race: Negro.
Mother's Maiden Name: Eliza Williams, age: 36.
Race: Negro.
Original Birth Certificate filed in Lancaster County on April 6, 1918.

126. Location of Birth: Co.: Lancaster; District: not given; Town: Litwalton.
Full Name of Child: Emma Laksie **Miles**.
Date of Birth: February 3, 1916.
Father's Name: James Miles, age: 41, occupation: farmer.
Race: Col. [Colored]
Mother's Maiden Name: Eliza Williams, age: 33.
Race: Col. [Colored]
Delayed Birth Certificate filed with the state registrar on October 2, 1933.

---

[35] At the bottom of this birth certificate, it states, "Given name added from a supplemental report, Mother." It is dated 1933.

127. Location of Birth: Co.: Lancaster; District: White Chapel; Town: Molusk.
Full Name of Child: Warren **Miles**.
Date of Birth: August 16, 1917.
Father's Name: William Miles, age: 27, occupation: day laborer.
Race: Negro.
Mother's Maiden Name: Elizabeth Fallin, age: 25.
Race: Negro.
Original Birth Certificate filed in Lancaster County on September 10, 1917.

128. Location of Birth: Co.: Lancaster; District: White Chapel; Town: not given.
Full Name of Child: Louis Peirce **Miller**.
Date of Birth: March 21, 1909.
Father's Name: T. F. Miller, age: 20, occupation: blacksmith.
Race: White.
Mother's Maiden Name: Mary Eva Stevens, age: 17.
Race: White.
Delayed Birth Certificate filed with the state registrar July 15, 1939.[36]

129. Location of Birth: Co.: Lancaster; District: not given; Town: Lively.
Full Name of Child: Collin Walker **Norris**.
Date of Birth: August 22, 1917.
Father's Name: Howard Allen Norris, age: 22, occupation: hauling.
Race: White.
Mother's Maiden Name: Sarah Elizabeth Walker, age: 18.
Race: White.
Delayed Birth Certificate filed with the state registrar on March 13, 1942.

130. Location of Birth: Co.: Lancaster; District: White Chapel; Town: Molusk.
Full Name of Child: Harold Francis **O'Brien**.
Date of Birth: March 7, 1918.
Father's Name: John O'Brien, age: 41, occupation: day laborer.
Race: White.
Mother's Maiden Name: Bessie Miller, age: 35.
Race: White.
Original Birth Certificate filed in Lancaster County on April 6, 1918.

131. Location of Birth: Co.: Lancaster; District: not given; Town: Nuttsville.
Full Name of Child: Alice Clark **Peirce**.
Date of Birth: January 22, 1902.
Father's Name: Joseph Peirce, age: 36, occupation: farmer.
Race: White.
Mother's Maiden Name: Janet Colquhoun Gilliam, age: 28.
Race: White.
Delayed Birth Certificate filed with the state registrar on January 30, 1953.

---

[36] There is another filing date for this birth with the County of Lancaster dated July 10, 1939.

132. Location of Birth: Co.: Lancaster; District: not given; Town: Nuttsville.
Full Name of Child: Chichester Tapscott **Peirce**, Jr.
Date of Birth: November 4, 1909.
Father's Name: C. T. Peirce, MD [Sr.], age: 32, occupation: medical doctor.
Race: White.
Mother's Maiden Name: Elizabeth Edrington Combs, age: 24.
Race: White.
Delayed Birth Certificate filed with the state registrar on August 24, 1942.

133. Location of Birth: Co.: Lancaster; District: not given; Town: Nuttsville.
Full Name of Child: Elizabeth Edrington **Peirce**.
Date of Birth: October 13, 1907.
Father's Name: Chichester Tapscott Peirce [Sr.], age: 30, occupation: physician.
Race: White.
Mother's Maiden Name: Elizabeth Edrington Combs, age: 22.
Race: White.
Delayed Birth Certificate filed with the state registrar on November 4, 1957.

134. Location of Birth: Co.: Lancaster; District: not given; Town: Nuttsville.
Full Name of Child: Flemintine Ball **Peirce**.
Date of Birth: September 26, 1904.
Father's Name: Joseph Peirce, age: 37, occupation: farmer.
Race: White.
Mother's Maiden Name: Janet Colquhoun Gilliam, age: 29.
Race: White.
Delayed Birth Certificate filed with the state registrar on April 8, 1954.

135. Location of Birth: Co.: Lancaster; District: White Chapel; Town: not given.
Full Name of Child: Katharine Moore **Peirce**.
Date of Birth: July 12, 1912.
Father's Name: Chichester T. Peirce [Sr.], age: 34, occupation: physician.
Race: White.
Mother's Maiden Name: Elizabeth E. Combs, age: 27.
Race: White.
Original Birth Certificate filed in Lancaster County on July 31, 1912.[37]

136. Location of Birth: Co.: Lancaster; District: White Chapel; Town: Nuttsville.
Full Name of Child: Addison Reginald **Pittman**.
Date of Birth: September 1, 1919.
Father's Name: A. R. Pittman, age: 32, occupation: farmer.
Race: White.
Mother's Maiden Name: Emma Taft, age: 26.
Race: White.
Original Birth Certificate filed in Lancaster County October 7, 1919.

[37] The words "Death Certificate" followed by a number are written at the top of this birth certificate. This child died December 29, 1914, according to a grave marker at St. Mary's Whitechapel Episcopal Church as recorded in Margaret Lester Hill & Clyde H. Ratcliffe, *In Remembrance...*, pub. 2002, p. 145.

137. Location of Birth: Co.: Lancaster; District: not given; Town: Regina.
     Full Name of Child: Edna Irene **Pittman**.
     Date of Birth: March 2, 1904.
     Father's Name: David Claiborn Pittman, age: 22, occupation: farmer.
     Race: White.
     Mother's Maiden Name: Sarah Elizabeth Davenport, age: 22.
     Race: White.
     Delayed Birth Certificate filed with the state registrar on April 18, 1957.

138. Location of Birth: Co.: Lancaster; District: not given; Town: Millenbeck.
     Full Name of Child: Laurence Edward **Pritchett**.
     Date of Birth: November 11, 1910.
     Father's Name: Charles Pritchett, age: 51, occupation: farming.
     Race: White.
     Mother's Maiden Name: Myrtine Saunders, age: 38.
     Race: White.
     Delayed Birth Certificate filed with the state registrar on May 10, 1941.

139. Location of Birth: Co.: Lancaster; District: White Chapel; Town: Bertrand.
     Full Name of Child: Susie Elizabeth **Radcliffe**.
     Date of Birth: March 17, 1919.
     Father's Name: T. F. Radcliffe, age: 58, occupation: oyster dealer.
     Race: White.
     Mother's Maiden Name: Annie Reynolds, age: 34.
     Race: White.
     Original Birth Certificate filed in Lancaster County April 15, 1919.

140. Location of Birth: Co.: Lancaster; District: White Chapel; Town: Alfonso.
     Full Name of Child: Elmer Wharton **Ramsey**.
     Date of Birth: August 23, 1913.
     Father's Name: Elmer Milton Ramsey, age: 40, occupation: preaching.
     Race: White.
     Mother's Maiden Name: Ruth Wharton, age: 25.
     Race: White.
     Original Birth Certificate filed in Lancaster County on September 11, 1913.

141. Location of Birth: Co.: Lancaster; District: White Chapel; Town: Litwalton.
     Full Name of Child: Mabel **Ransome**.
     Date of Birth: July 4, 1912.
     Father's Name: S.W. Ransome, age: 46, occupation: farmer & oysterman.
     Race: Black.
     Mother's Maiden Name: Mary Laws, age: 31.
     Race: Negro.
     Original Birth Certificate filed in Lancaster County on August 10, 1912.

142. Location of Birth: Co.: Lancaster; District: White Chapel; Town: Litwalton.
Full Name of Child: Walter Spicer **Ransome**.
Date of Birth: April 1, 1916.
Father's Name: S. W. Ransome, age: 54, occupation: day laborer.
Race: Col. [Colored].
Mother's Maiden Name: Gertrude Laws, age: 36.
Race: Col. [Colored].
Delayed Birth Certificate filed with the local registrar on August 31, 1942.

143. Location of Birth: Co.: Lancaster; District: White Chapel; Town: Ottoman.
Full Name of Child: Francis Gordon **Ransone**.
Date of Birth: March 19, 1919.
Father's Name: John Ransone, age: 37, occupation: farmer.
Race: White.
Mother's Maiden Name: Dora Ketner, age: 39.
Race: White.
Original Birth Certificate filed in Lancaster County April 15, 1919.

144. Location of Birth: Co.: Lancaster; District: White Chapel; Town: Litwalton.
Full Name of Child: Annie Fitzhugh **Revere.**
Date of Birth: June 13, 1913.
Father's Name: John Revere, age: 30, occupation: not given.
Race: White.
Mother's Maiden Name: Mary Sipes, age: 24.
Race: White.
Original Birth Certificate filed in Lancaster County on July 9, 1913.

145. Location of Birth: Co.: Lancaster; District: White Chapel; Town: Molusk.
Full Name of Child: Torvilla Bryan **Revere** [female child].
Date of Birth: March 22, 1916.
Father's Name: John Revere, age: 33, occupation: farmer.
Race: White.
Mother's Maiden Name: Mary Sipes, age: 28.
Race: White.
Original Birth Certificate filed in Lancaster County on April 4, 1916.

146. Location of Birth: Co.: Lancaster, District: not given; Town: Lively.
Full Name of Child: Leon Hugh **Rice**.
Date of Birth: October 2, 1911.
Father's Name: Lawrence Hugh Rice, age: 22, occupation: salesman.
Race: White.
Mother's Maiden Name: Essie Claybrook Revere, age: 22.
Race: White.
Delayed Birth Certificate filed with the state registrar on December 20, 1955.

147. Location of Birth: Co.: Lancaster, District: Mantua; Town: Lively.
     Full Name of Child: Nell Elizabeth **Rice**.
     Date of Birth: January 10, 1915.
     Father's Name: Lawrence Rice, age: 25, occupation: traveling salesman.
     Race: White.
     Mother's Maiden Name: Ethel Revere, age: 25.
     Race: White.
     Original Birth Certificate filed in Lancaster County on April 2, 1915.

148. Location of Birth: Co.: Lancaster; District: not given; Town: Nuttsville.
     Full Name of Child: Mildred Elizabeth **Roane**.
     Date of Birth: September 17, 1908.[38]
     Father's Name: James Landon Roane, age: 29, occupation: farmer.
     Race: Negro.
     Mother's Maiden Name: Lelia Frances Redmond, age: 22.
     Race: Negro.
     Delayed Birth Certificate filed with the state registrar on April 8, 1955.

149. Location of Birth: Co.: Lancaster; District: White Chapel; Town: Molusk.
     Full Name of Child: William Norman **Roane**.
     Date of Birth: February 12, 1916.
     Father's Name: Landon Roane, age: 37, occupation: oysterman.
     Race: Negro.
     Mother's Maiden Name: Lelia Redman, age: 27.
     Race: Negro.
     Original Birth Certificate filed in Lancaster County on March 10, 1916.

150. Location of Birth: Co.: Lancaster; District: White Chapel; Town: Ottoman.
     Full Name of Child: Hazel Hunter **Russell.**
     Date of Birth: November 5, 1918.
     Father's Name: Raymond Russell, age: 49, occupation: farmer.
     Race: White.
     Mother's Maiden Name: Susie Grover, age: 46.
     Race: White.
     Delayed Birth Certificate filed in Lancaster County on April 27, 1926.

151. Location of Birth: Co.: Lancaster; District: White Chapel; Town: Monaskon.
     Full Name of Child: Thomas Mathew **Sanford**.[39]
     Date of Birth: October 27, 1917.
     Father's Name: H. B. Sanford, age: 33, occupation: traveling salesman.
     Race: White.
     Mother's Maiden Name: Katherine Taylor, age: 32.
     Race: White.
     Original Birth Certificate filed in Lancaster County on November 10, 1917.

---

[38] At the bottom of this birth certificate, it states, "Dr. C. T. Peirce states that the date of birth of Mildred Elizabeth Roane (September 17, 1908) was taken from his private records."

[39] At the bottom of the birth certificate, it states, "Given name added from a supplemental report," and it is dated January 3, 1918. At the top of the birth certificate is written "Died 11-11-17," referring to the baby.

152. Location of Birth: Co.: Lancaster; District: White Chapel; Town: Molusk.
Full Name of Child: Albert **Saunders**.
Date of Birth: February 16, 1917.
Father's Name: Gerome Saunders, age: 26, occupation: day laborer.
Race: Negro.
Mother's Maiden Name: Elsie Waites, age: 24.
Race: Negro.
Original Birth Certificate filed in Lancaster County on March 10, 1917.

153. Location of Birth: Co.: Lancaster; District: White Chapel; Town: not given.
Full Name of Child: Elleck [crossed out and written Alex] Linwood
Saunders.[40]
Date of Birth: May 30, 1913.
Father's Name: Frank W. Saunders, age: 47, occupation: farmer.
Race: White.
Mother's Maiden Name: Janie Bruer, age: 44.
Race: White.
Original Birth Certificate filed in Lancaster County on June 6, 1913.

154. Location of Birth: Co.: Lancaster; District: White Chapel; Town: Molusk.
Full Name of Child: Spencer Warren **Saunders**.
Date of Birth: May 26, 1917.
Father's Name: Sullivan Saunders, age: 23, occupation: day laborer.
Race: White.
Mother's Maiden Name: Lydia George, age: 18.
Race: White.
Original Birth Certificate filed in Lancaster County on June 16, 1917.

155. Location of Birth: Co.: Lancaster; District: not given; Town: Millenbeck.
Full Name of Child: Samuel Horace **Scott**.
Date of Birth: August 28, 1910.
Father's Name: Thomas Scott, age: 37, occupation: waterman.
Race: White.
Mother's Maiden Name: Sadie Bell Olliver, age: 28.
Race: White.
Delayed Birth Certificate filed with the state registrar on April 16, 1953.

156. Location of Birth: Co.: Lancaster; District: White Chapel; Town: Molusk.
Full Name of Child: Cora Anna **Seawell**.
Date of Birth: August 30, 1916.
Father's Name: B. F. Seawell, age: 29, occupation: day laborer.
Race: White.
Mother's Maiden Name: Hattie Whealton, age: 35.
Race: White.
Original Birth Certificate filed in Lancaster County on September 11, 1916.

---

[40] At the bottom of this birth certificate, it states, "Given name added from a supplemental record from applicant." It is dated June 19, 1944.

157. Location of Birth: Co.: Lancaster; District: not given; Town: Lively.
Full Name of Child: Sadie Blanch **Slater**.
Date of Birth: October 29, 1913.
Father's Name: Benj. Franklin Slater, age: 23, occupation: day laborer.
Race: White.
Mother's Maiden Name: Sadie Blanch Haynie, age: 19.
Race: White.
Original Birth Certificate filed in Lancaster County on November 1, 1913.

158. Location of Birth: Co.: Lancaster; District: White Chapel; Town: Nuttsville.
Full Name of Child: Harvey/Harry **Smith**.
Date of Birth: March 28, 1917.
Father's Name: Buoy Smith, age: 25, occupation: day laborer.
Race: Negro.
Mother's Maiden Name: Ada Branham, age: 26.
Race: Negro.
Original Birth Certificate filed in Lancaster County on April 11, 1917.

159. Location of Birth: Co.: Lancaster; District: White Chapel; Town: Molusk.
Full Name of Child: Martha Maglene **Smith**. [#1 of a set of twins; see record 160.]
Date of Birth: March 16, 1919.
Father's Name: Ulyses [Ulysses] Smith, age: 24, occupation: not given.
Race: Colored.
Mother's Maiden Name: Edna Johnson, age: 19.
Race: Colored.
Original Birth Certificate filed in Lancaster County March 25, 1919.

160. Location of Birth: Co.: Lancaster; District: White Chapel; Town: Molusk.
Full Name of Child: Mary Aliene **Smith**. [#2 of a set of twins; see record 159.]
Date of Birth: March 16, 1919.
Father's Name: Ulyses [Ulysses] Smith, age: 24, occupation: not given.
Race: Colored.
Mother's Maiden Name: Edna Johnson, age: 19.
Race: Colored.
Original Birth Certificate filed in Lancaster County March 25, 1919.

161. Location of Birth: Co.: Lancaster; District: Mantua; Town: Lively.
Full Name of Child: William Ernest **Taft**.
Date of Birth: January 21, 1918.
Father's Name: O. F. Taft, age: 31, occupation: carpenter.
Race: W [White].
Mother's Maiden Name: Sadie Irene Norris, age: 29.
Race: W [White].
Delayed Birth Certificate filed in Lancaster County on July 23, 1941.

162. Location of Birth: Co.: Lancaster; District: White Chapel; Town: Molusk.
Full Name of Child: Daisey Elizabeth **Taylor**.
Date of Birth: October 18, 1916.
Father's Name: Harry Taylor, age: 22, occupation: day laborer.
Race: White.
Mother's Maiden Name: Daisey Hutchins, age: 22.
Race: White.
Original Birth Certificate filed in Lancaster County on November 14, 1916.

163. Location of Birth: Co.: Lancaster; District: White Chapel; Town: Litwalton.
Full Name of Child: Edwin Marcellus **Thomas**.
Date of Birth: July 25, 1907.
Father's Name: Frank Thomas, age: 40, occupation: day laborer.
Race: White.
Mother's Maiden Name: Gertrude Cannon, age: 31.
Race: White.
Delayed Birth Certificate filed with the state registrar on November 26,1940.[41]

164. Location of Birth: Co.: Lancaster; District: White Chapel; Town: Molusk.
Full Name of Child: Esther Elisabeth **Thomas**.[42]
Date of Birth: November 1, 1916.
Father's Name: B. W. Thomas, age: 37, occupation: oyster dealer.
Race: White.
Mother's Maiden Name: Blanch E. Grove, age: 30.
Race: White.
Original Birth Certificate filed in Lancaster County on November 14, 1916.

165. Location of Birth: Co.: Lancaster; District: White Chapel; Town: Ottoman.
Full Name of Child: Mary Eliza **Thomas**.
Date of Birth: July 27, 1919.
Father's Name: J. W. Thomas, age: 47, occupation: carpenter.
Race: White.
Mother's Maiden Name: Clementine Belfield, age: 33.
Race: White.
Original Birth Certificate filed in Lancaster County May 13, 1920.

166. Location of Birth: Co.: Lancaster; District: White Chapel; Town: Molusk.
Full Name of Child: Ruth Duvall **Thomas**.
Date of Birth: October 4, 1915.
Father's Name: Benjamin W. Thomas, age: 35, occupation: oyster dealer.
Race: White.
Mother's Maiden Name: Blanch Grove, age: 28.
Race: White.
Original Birth Certificate filed in Lancaster County on November 9, 1915.

---

[41] There is a second filing date with the local registrar dated November 23, 1940.
[42] At the bottom of this birth certificate, it states, "Given name added from a supplemental report." It was dated March 16, 1917.

167. Location of Birth: Co.: Lancaster; District: White Chapel; Town: Molusk.
Full Name of Child: Dora **Thompson**.[43]
Date of Birth: September 8, 1918.
Father's Name: Philip Thomas, age: 39, occupation: day laborer.
Race: Negro.
Mother's Maiden Name: Febe Waites, age: 30.
Race: Negro.
Original Birth Certificate filed in Lancaster County on September 21, 1918.

168. Location of Birth: Co.: Lancaster; District: not given; Town: Morattico.
Full Name of Child: James Hannibal **Thrift**.
Date of Birth: October 22, 1906.
Father's Name: Littleton C. Thrift, age: 33, occupation: farmer.
Race: White.
Mother's Maiden Name: Mary Viola Sparrow, age: 20.
Race: White.
Delayed Birth Certificate filed with the state registrar on February 3, 1958.

169. Location of Birth: Co.: Lancaster; District: White Chapel; Town: Molusk.
Full Name of Child: Buddy Grant **Waits**.
Date of Birth: March 18, 1915.
Father's Name: Emanuel Waits, age: 50, occupation: day laborer.
Race: Negro.
Mother's Maiden Name: Sedonia Kelley, age: 42.
Race: Negro.
Original Birth Certificate filed in Lancaster County on April 1, 1915.

170. Location of Birth: Co.: Lancaster; District: White Chapel; Town: Litwalton.
Full Name of Child: Howard Vernon **Waits**.
Date of Birth: March 21, 1913.
Father's Name: Emanuel Waits, age: 49, occupation: day laborer.
Race: Negro.
Mother's Maiden Name: Sedonia Kelley, age: 38.
Race: Negro.
Original Birth Certificate filed in Lancaster County on April 18, 1913.

171. Location of Birth: Co.: Lancaster; District: White Chapel; Town: Alfonso.
Full Name of Child: Alexander C. **Walker**.
Date of Birth: March 25, 1917.
Father's Name: A. C. Walker, age: 29, occupation: clergyman.
Race: White.
Mother's Maiden Name: Maude Ashley, age: 26.
Race: White.
Original Birth Certificate filed in Lancaster County on April 11, 1917.

---

[43] At the bottom of this birth certificate, it states, "Given name added from a supplemental report." It was dated October 5, 1951.

172. Location of Birth: Co.: Lancaster; District: not given; Town: Ottoman.
Full Name of Child: James Westley **Walker**.
Date of Birth: December 3, 1910.
Father's Name: T. W. Walker, age: 25, occupation: farmer.
Race: White.
Mother's Maiden Name: Mary Maggie Haywood, age: 21.
Race: White.
Delayed Birth Certificate filed with the state registrar on June 18, 1941.

173. Location of Birth: Co.: Lancaster; District: White Chapel; Town: Nuttsville.
Full Name of Child: Eaula **Walters**.[44]
Date of Birth: March 26, 1917.
Father's Name: Alfred Walters, age: 38, occupation: day laborer.
Race: Negro.
Mother's Maiden Name: Mary Tolliaferro, age: 30.
Race: Negro.
Original Birth Certificate filed in Lancaster County on April 11, 1917.

174. Location of Birth: Co.: Lancaster; District: White Chapel; Town: Nuttsville.
Full Name of Child: Evelyn Nebith **Warring**.
Date of Birth: October 5, 1913.
Father's Name: John Warring, age: 39, occupation: farmer.
Race: Negro.
Mother's Maiden Name: Annie Mitchell, age: 31.
Race: Negro.
Original Birth Certificate filed in Lancaster County on October 8, 1913.

175. Location of Birth: Co.: Lancaster; District: White Chapel; Town: Molusk.
Full Name of Child: John Henry **Warring**.
Date of Birth: November 19, 1915.
Father's Name: John Henry Warring, age: 40, occupation: oysterman.
Race: Colored.
Mother's Maiden Name: Annie Mitchell, age: 34.
Race: Colored.
Original Birth Certificate filed in Lancaster County on January 31, 1916.

176. Location of Birth: Co.: Lancaster; District: White Chapel; Town: Molusk.
Full Name of Child: Julian Ford **Warwick**.
Date of Birth: March 28, 1916.
Father's Name: Beatles Warwick, age: 41, occupation: lumber mfgr.
Race: White.
Mother's Maiden Name: Julia Elmore, age: 37.
Race: White.
Original Birth Certificate filed in Lancaster County on May 10, 1916.

---

[44] Beside the child's name are the words, "Died 5-5-1917."

177. Location of Birth: Co.: Lancaster; District: White Chapel; Town: not given.
Full Name of Child: Hattie Rubinette **Weaver**.
Date of Birth: September 2, 1912.
Father's Name: William Arville Weaver, age: 50, occupation: carpenter & farmer.
Race: Colored.
Mother's Maiden Name: Hattie May Wiggins, age: 29.
Race: Colored.
Original Birth Certificate filed in Lancaster County on September 13, 1912.

178. Location of Birth: Co.: Lancaster; District: White Chapel; Town: Molusk.
Full Name of Child: Virginia Eloise **Weaver**.
Date of Birth: November 23, 1915.
Father's Name: Elmore Weaver, age: 28, occupation: oysterman.
Race: Colored.
Mother's Maiden Name: Josephine Waits, age: 25.
Original Birth Certificate filed in Lancaster County on January 31, 1916.

179. Location of Birth: Co.: Lancaster; District: not given; Town: Lively.
Full Name of Child: Grace Helen **Webb**.
Date of Birth: January 16, 1900.
Father's Name: Benjamin Franklin Webb, age: 39, occupation: not given.
Race: White.
Mother's Maiden Name: Sarah Lena Barker, age: 30.
Race: White.
Delayed Birth Certificate filed with state registrar on November 20, 1945. [45]

180. Location of Birth: Co.: Lancaster; District: not given; Town: Lively.
Full Name of Child: Hilda Elsie **Webb**.
Date of Birth: February 2, 1910.
Father's Name: Benjamin Franklin Webb, age: 49, occupation: not given.
Race: White.
Mother's Maiden Name: Sarah Lena Barker, age: 40.
Race: White.
Delayed Birth Certificate filed with state registrar on November 20, 1945.

181. Location of Birth: Co.: Lancaster; District: Mantua; Town: Lively.
Full Name of Child: Linda Burton **Webb**.[46]
Date of Birth: September 27, 1913.
Father's Name: Franklin Barker Webb, age: 22, occupation: day laborer.
Race: White.
Mother's Maiden Name: Bessie Alvey Brown, age: 22.
Race: White.
Original Birth Certificate filed in Lancaster County on November 1, 1913.

---

[45] See image on page viii.
[46] At the bottom of this birth certificate, it states, "Given name added from a supplemental report." It is dated March 17, 1914.

182. Location of Birth: Co.: Lancaster; District: Mantua; Town: Lively.
     Full Name of Child: Marian Elaine **Webb**.[47]
     Date of Birth: October 4, 1912.
     Father's Name: B. F. Webb, age: 51, occupation: farmer.
     Race: White.
     Mother's Maiden Name: Sarah L. Barker, age: 41.
     Race: White.
     Original Birth Certificate filed in Lancaster County on October 5, 1912.

183. Location of Birth: Co.: Lancaster; District: Mantua; Town: Lively.
     Full Name of Child: Ruby Beatrice **Webb**.
     Date of Birth: April 3, 1903.
     Father's Name: B. F. Webb, age: 40, occupation: farmer.
     Race: White.
     Mother's Maiden Name: Sarah Lena Barker, age: 31.
     Race: White.
     Delayed Birth Certificate filed with the state registrar on Sept. 24, 1940.[48]

184. Location of Birth: Co.: Lancaster; District: White Chapel; Town: Litwalton.
     Full Name of Child: John Howard **Whay**.
     Date of Birth: May 2, 1913.
     Father's Name: Luther Whay, age: 36, occupation: day laborer.
     Race: White.
     Mother's Maiden Name: Kate Edwards, age: 23.
     Race: White.
     Original Birth Certificate filed in Lancaster County on June 6, 1913.

185. Location of Birth: Co.: Lancaster; District: White Chapel; Town: Litwalton.
     Full Name of Child: Ricisse Roshill **Whay** [male child].
     Date of Birth: April 10, 1917.
     Father's Name: Luther Whay, age: 43, occupation: was day laborer.
     Race: White.
     Maiden Name: Kate Edwards, age: 27.
     Mother's Race: White.
     Original Birth Certificate filed in Lancaster County on April 20, 1917.

186. Location of Birth: Co.: Lancaster; District: White Chapel; Town: Molusk.
     Full Name of Child: Frances Fauntleroy **Williams**.
     Date of Birth: February 13, 1915.
     Father's Name: Fred Williams, age: 32, occupation: day laborer.
     Race: Negro.
     Mother's Maiden Name: Sarah Fauntleroy, age: 29.
     Race: Negro.
     Original Birth Certificate filed in Lancaster County on March 1, 1915.

---

[47] At the bottom of this birth certificate, it states, "Given name added from affidavit and a record in B. V. S." It is dated December 2, 1964. At the top of this birth certificate is written "Amended."

[48] There is a filing date with the local registrar of September 23, 1940.

187. Location of Birth: Co.: Lancaster; District: White Chapel; Town: Molusk.
Full Name of Child: Thomas Emory **Williams**.
Date of Birth: January 14, 1917.
Father's Name: Frederick Williams, age:35, occupation: oysterman.
Race: Colored.
Mother's Maiden Name: Sarah Fauntleroy, age: 31.
Race: Colored.
Original Birth Certificate filed in Lancaster County on February 7, 1917.

188. Location of Birth: Co.: Lancaster; District: White Chapel; Town: Molusk.
Full Name of Child: Ira Bennett **Wingate** [one of a set of twins; see record 189].
Date of Birth: March 13, 1918.
Father's Name: William Wingate, age: 44, occupation: merchant.
Race: White.
Mother's Maiden Name: Lennie Wilcox, age: 28.
Race: White.
Original Birth Certificate filed in Lancaster County on April 6, 1918.

189. Location of Birth: Co.: Lancaster; District: White Chapel; Town: Molusk.
Full Name of Child: Irving Napoleon Bonaparte **Wingate** [one of a set of twins; see record 188].
Date of Birth: March 13, 1918.
Father's Name: William B. Wingate, age: 44, occupation: merchant.
Race: White.
Mother's Maiden Name: Lennie Wilcox, age: 28.
Race: White.
Original Birth Certificate filed in Lancaster County on April 6, 1918.

190. Location of Birth: Co.: Lancaster; District: White Chapel; Town: Molusk.
Full Name of Child: Margaret Willcox **Wingate**.
Date of Birth: July 17, 1919.
Father's Name: William B. Wingate, age: 46, occupation: merchant.
Race: White.
Mother's Maiden Name: Linnie Willcox, age: 31.
Race: White.
Original Birth Certificate filed in Lancaster County August 9, 1919.

191. Location of Birth: Co.: Lancaster; District: White Chapel; Town: Millenbeck.
Full Name of Child: Emma Lee **Wist**.[49]
Date of Birth: April 6, 1919.
Father's Name: John Wist, age: 24, occupation: day laborer.
Race: White.
Mother's Maiden Name: Hannah Hutchins, age: 24.
Race: White.
Original Birth Certificate filed in Lancaster County April 15, 1919.

---

[49] Written beside the child's name on the birth certificate is a statement saying, "Died June 1919."

192. Location of Birth: Co.: Lancaster; District: Mantua; Town: Alfonso.
Full Name of Child: Robert Claybrook **Wood**.[50]
Date of Birth: August 7, 1912.
Father's Name: Albert D. Wood, age: 51, occupation: farmer.
Race: Black.
Mother's Maiden Name: Eliza Cambel, age: 32.
Race: Black.
Original Birth Certificate filed in Lancaster County on August 12, 1912.

The following Lancaster County birth records are those of the children who were not named at the time of birth. On these birth certificates, the line for "Full Name of Child" is left blank. US Census records in Lancaster County, Virginia, as well as cemetery records have been searched to help identify these children. Census records were not found for those not cited in a footnote.

193. Location of Birth: Co.: Lancaster; District: White Chapel; Town: Molusk.
Full Name of Child: Baby girl not named.
Date of Birth: January 24, 1916.
Father's Name: James Henry **Croxton**, age: 38, occupation: oysterman.
Race: Colored.
Mother's Maiden Name: Martha Lewis, age: 36.
Race: Colored.
Original Birth Certificate filed in Lancaster County January 31, 1916.

194. Location of Birth: Co.: Lancaster; District: Mantua; Town: not given.
Full Name of Child: "Unnamed **Davenport**"[51]
The birth certificate states this child is a girl.
Date of Birth: August 9, 1913.
Father's Name: Hidey Davenport, age: 27, occupation: day laborer.
Race: Negro.
Mother's Maiden Name: Mattie Wood, age: 25.
Race: Negro.
Original Birth Certificate filed in Lancaster County August 16, 1913.

---

[50] At the bottom of the birth certificate, it states, "Given name added from a supplemental report." This is dated September 7, 1912.
[51] There are no census records in Lancaster County, VA for this family in 1920. The 1930 US Census for Lancaster County shows this family with a daughter named Olean Davenport, age 16 who could be this child.

195. Location of Birth: Co.: Lancaster; District: Mantua; Town: Lara.
     Full Name of Child: Baby boy not named.[52]
     Date of Birth: September 14, 1913.
     Father's Name: Howard **Davenport**, age: 49, occupation: farmer.
     Race: White.
     Mother's Maiden Name: Bettie Alice Rice, age: 42.
     Race: White.
     Original Birth Certificate filed in Lancaster County November 1, 1913.

196. Location of Birth: Co.: Lancaster; District: Mantua; Town: Alfonso.
     Full Name of Child: Baby girl not named.[53]
     Date of Birth: June 14, 1917.
     Father's Name: Raney **Davenport**, age: 26, occupation: day laborer.
     Race: Negro.
     Mother's Maiden Name: Grace Conaway, age: 25.
     Race: Negro.
     Original Birth Certificate filed in Lancaster County June 16, 1917.

197. Location of Birth: Co.: Lancaster; District: White Chapel; Town: Molusk.
     Full Name of Child: Baby boy not named.[54]
     Date of Birth: December 24, 1915.
     Father's Name: Lumbard **Dawson**, age: 32, occupation: day laborer.
     Race: White.
     Mother's Maiden Name: Bessie Enos, age: 45.
     Race: White.
     Original Birth Certificate filed in Lancaster County January 31, 1916.

198. Location of Birth: Co.: Lancaster; District: White Chapel; Town: Boer.
     Full Name of Child: Baby boy not named.
     Date of Birth: September 21, 1913.
     Father's Name: James **Dixon**, age: 37, occupation: day laborer.
     Race: Negro.
     Mother's Maiden Name: Lucy Chowning, age: 38.
     Race: Negro.
     Original Birth Certificate filed in Lancaster County September 30, 1913.

---

[52] The 1920 US Census shows this family in Richmond County, Farnham District with a boy named H. Franklin Davenport, age 6 who could be this child.

[53] There is no information on this family in Lancaster County in the 1920 US Census. The 1930 US Census shows this family in Lancaster County with a daughter named Marian Davenport, age 12 who could be this child.

[54] There is no information on this family in Lancaster County in the 1920 US Census. The 1930 US Census shows this family in Lancaster County, White Chapel District with a boy named Lyell Dawson, age 14 who could be this child.

199. Location of Birth: Co.: Lancaster; District: White Chapel; Town: not given.
Full Name of Child: Baby boy not named.
Date of Birth: September 1, 1917.
Father's Name: James **Dixon**, age: not given, occupation: day laborer.
Race: Negro.
Mother's Maiden Name: Cilia Towles, age: 19.
Race: Negro.
Original Birth Certificate filed in Lancaster County November 10, 1917.

200. Location of Birth: Co.: Lancaster; District: Mantua; Town: not given.
Full Name of Child: Baby boy not named.[55]
Date of Birth: July 18, 1912.
Father's Name: J. M. **Haynie**, age: 37, occupation: farmer and blacksmith.
Race: White.
Mother's Maiden Name: Viola Marsh, age: 35.
Race: White.
Original Birth Certificate filed in Lancaster County July (no date), 1912.

201. Location of Birth: Co.: Lancaster; District: Mantua; Town: Lively.
Full Name of Child: Baby boy not named.
Date of Birth: September 21, 1913.
Father's Name: Arthur **Polk**, age: 50, occupation: day laborer.
Race: Negro.
Mother's Maiden Name: Bertina Curry, age: 32.
Race: Negro.
Original Birth Certificate filed in Lancaster County September 22, 1913.

202. Location of Birth: Co.: Lancaster; District: White Chapel; Town: Nuttsville.
Full Name of Child: Baby boy not named.[56]
Date of Birth: October 2, 1913.
Father's Name: Landon **Roane**, age: 39, occupation: farmer.
Race: Negro.
Mother's Maiden Name: Lilia Redman, age: 37.
Race: Negro.
Original Birth Certificate filed in Lancaster County October 8, 1913.

203. Location of Birth: Co.: Lancaster; District: White Chapel; Town: Molusk.
Full Name of Child: Baby girl not named.
Date of Birth: January 28, 1915.
Father's Name: Nearwood **Robinson**, age: 26, occupation: oyster shucker.
Race: Negro.
Mother's Maiden Name: Lena Harmonson, age: 26; occupation: oyster shucker.
Race: Negro.
Original Birth Certificate filed in Lancaster County March 1, 1915.

---

[55] Through findagrave.com, the cemetery records of Lebanon Baptist Church in Lancaster County show the grave of Andrew Haynie born and died July 18, 1912. His parents were John Morgan Haynie and Sadie Viola Marsh Haynie.
[56] The 1920 US Census for Lancaster County, VA White Chapel District shows this family with a boy named Carter Roane, age 7 who could be this child.

204. Location of Birth: Co.: Lancaster; District: White Chapel; Town: Litwalton.
Full Name of Child: Baby boy not named [Birth Certificate says "unnamed
Smith"].
Date of Birth: December 8, 1912.
Father's Name: "Can't ascertain unknown." No facts are known about the
father other than he was an African American [Birth Certificate says
"Black"].
Mother's Maiden Name: Jinny **Smith**, age: unknown, occupation: house
servant.[57]
Original Birth Certificate filed in Lancaster County December 14, 1912.

205. Location of Birth: Co.: Lancaster; District: White Chapel; Town: Alfonso.
Full Name of Child: Unnamed girl **Smith**.
Date of Birth: April 10, 1919.
Father's Name: John **Smith**, age: 34, occupation: day laborer.
Race: Negro.
Mother's Maiden Name: Matty Taylor, age: 33.
Race: Negro.
Original Birth Certificate filed in Lancaster County April 12, 1919.

206. Location of Birth: Co.: Lancaster; District: White Chapel; Town: Molusk.
Full Name of Child: Baby boy not named.[58]
Date of Birth: October 4, 1916.
Father's Name: **Strang**, David A., age: 40 [born ca. 1876], occupation:
editor.
Race: White.
Mother's Maiden Name: Laura S. Dardwell, age: 36.
Race: White.
Original Birth Certificate filed in Lancaster County November 14, 1916.

207. Location of Birth: Co.: Lancaster; District: Mantua; Town: Alfonso.
Full Name of Child: Baby girl not named.[59]
Date of Birth: May 31, 1917.
Father's Name: Youey **Waites**, age: 38, occupation: day laborer.
Race: Negro.
Mother's Maiden Name: Mary Wood, age: 25.
Race: Negro.
Original Birth Certificate filed in Lancaster County June 16, 1917.

---

[57] The 1900 US Census in Lancaster County White Chapel District shows a Jinnie Smith, age 22, born ca. 1888, African American, single, with one child named Olive, age 1. There is no information on her in the 1920 US Census with this child born in 1912.

[58] The child in this record is a third child. These parents had a set of twins born May 22, 1915: a girl, Laura Sax Smyth Strang, and a boy, David Alvin Strang [Jr.]. The daughter, Laura, died June 6, 1915, and is buried at St. Mary's Whitechapel Episcopal Church Cemetery. There are birth certificates for both twins, signed by Dr. Steuart of Ottoman. Those records name the parents as David Alvin Strang and Laura Sax Smyth.

[59] The 1920 US Census for Lancaster County, Mantua District shows this family with a daughter Lottie Waites, age 2 who could be this child.

NORTHUMBERLAND COUNTY, VIRGINIA, HOME BIRTHS ATTENDED BY DR. C. T. PEIRCE

1900 to 1919

All information and spellings are as they appear on the birth certificates. All birth records are listed in alphabetical order. Race is listed as it appears on the birth certificate.[60]

1. Location of Birth: Co.: Northumberland; District: Heathsville; Town: Miskimon.
   Full Name of Child: George Hinton **Beane**.[61]
   Date of Birth: August 19, 1918.
   Father's Name: T. S. Beane, age: 33, occupation: merchant.
   Race: White.
   Mother's Maiden Name: Grace Hinton, age: 24.
   Race: White.
   Original Birth Certificate filed in Northumberland County in August, 1918.

2. Location of Birth: Co.: Northumberland; District: Heathsville; Town: Miskimon.
   Full Name of Child: Mary Gertrude **Beane**.
   Date of Birth: May 27, 1913.
   Father's Name: George Milton Beane, age: 30, occupation: lumberman.
   Race: White.
   Mother's Maiden Name: Janie Gray Hall, age: 29.
   Race: White.
   Original Birth Certificate filed in Northumberland County on June 10, 1913.

3. Location of Birth: Co.: Northumberland; District: Heathsville; Town: Miskimon.
   Full Name of Child: Baby boy not named.[62]
   Date of Birth: January 27, 1917.
   Father's Name: No information given on the father.
   Mother's Maiden Name: Ida **Bee**, age: 20, occupation: house servant.
   Race: Negro.
   Original Birth Certificate filed in Northumberland County on June 10, 1917.

---

[60] Source for all images of birth certificates is Ancestry.com, *Virginia, U.S., Birth Records, 1912-2015, Delayed Birth Records, 1721-1920* [Original data: Virginia, Births, 1721–2015, Virginia Department of Health, Richmond, Virginia], accessed 2021-2022.

[61] At the bottom of the birth certificate, it states, "Given name added from a supplemental report." This is dated September 10, 1918 and signed J. T. Beane.

[62] There are no census records in 1920 in Northumberland County for this mother and child.

4. Location of Birth: Co.: Northumberland; District: Heathsville; Town: not given.
    Full Name of Child: James Everett **Davenport**.
    Date of Birth: February 28, 1910.
    Father's Name: A. B. Davenport, age: 33, occupation: farmer.
    Race: White.
    Mother's Maiden Name: Mary Elizabeth Luttrell, age: 26.
    Race: White.
    Delayed Birth Certificate filed with the state registrar November 11, 1939. [63]

5. Location of Birth: Co.: Northumberland; District: Heathsville; Town: Lara.
    Full Name of Child: John Webster **Davenport**.
    Date of Birth: September 20, 1904.
    Father's Name: A. B. Davenport, age: 27, occupation: farmer.
    Race: White.
    Mother's Maiden Name: Mary E. Luttrell, age: 29.
    Race: White.
    Delayed Birth Certificate filed with the state registrar September 30, 1941.

6. Location of Birth: Co.: Northumberland; District: Heathsville; Town: Lara.
    Full Name of Child: William Ray **Davenport**. [64]
    Date of Birth: April 25, 1917.
    Father's Name: W. B. Davenport, age: 45, occupation: farmer.
    Race: White.
    Mother's Maiden Name: Sofia Anne Rice, age: 44.
    Race: White.
    Original Birth Certificate filed in Northumberland County July 10, 1917.

7. Location of Birth: Co.: Northumberland; District: not given; Town: Litwalton. [65]
    Full Name of Child: Sarah Ann **Edwards**.
    Date of Birth: February 11, 1913.
    Father's Name: William Corbin Edwards, age: 21, occupation: laborer.
    Race: White.
    Mother's Maiden Name: Lessie [could be Lusie] Gertrude Cannon, age: 39.
    Race: White.
    Delayed Birth Certificate filed with the state registrar October 28, 1931.

---

[63] The birth certificate was also filed in Northumberland County on October 15, 1939.

[64] At the bottom of this birth certificate it states, "#2 [line 2 on the certificate], name added by affidavit and child's birth record." This is dated January 24, 1979 and initialed JM. The word "Amended" is added at the top of the birth certificate.

[65] Although the location of this birth is given as Litwalton, Litwalton is in Lancaster County, VA. Written on the back of the birth certificate is "Parents married May 13, 1912, Leabon [Lebanon] Parsonage, Lancaster County, Alfonso, Va." This would be Lebanon Baptist Church.

8. Location of Birth: Co.: Northumberland; District: Heathsville; Town: Miskimon.
    Full Name of Child: Elton James **Forrester.**
    Date of Birth: August 5, 1919.
    Father's Name: Elgin W. Forrester, age: 32, occupation: farmer.
    Race: White.
    Mother's Maiden Name: Mary Alice Gill, age: 32.
    Race: White.
    Original Birth Certificate filed in Northumberland County August 10, 1919.

9. Location of Birth: Co.: Northumberland; District: not given; Town: Miskimon.
    Full Name of Child: Ivis Leonard **Forrester**.
    Date of Birth: May 5, 1913.
    Father's Name: Ivis Lee Forrester, age: 24, occupation: farmer.
    Race: White.
    Mother's Maiden Name: Nannie Cora Revere, age: 29.
    Race: White.
    Original Birth Certificate filed in Northumberland County May 22, 1913.

10. Location of Birth: Co.: Northumberland; District: not given; Town: Farnham.[66]
    Full Name of Child: William Richard **Harris**, Jr.
    Date of Birth: August 2, 1915.
    Father's Name: W. R. Harris, Sr., age: 42, occupation: farmer.
    Race: White.
    Mother's Maiden Name: Eva Katherine Thomas, age: 31.
    Race: White.
    Delayed Birth Certificate filed with the state registrar December 15, 1941.

11. Location of Birth: Co.: Northumberland; District: not given; Town: Lara.
    Full Name of Child: Margaret Virginia **Hinton**.
    Date of Birth: October 9, 1908.
    Father's Name: Ira D. Hinton, age: 26, occupation: farmer.
    Race: White.
    Mother's Maiden Name: Ida Byrd Thomas, age: 26.
    Race: White.
    Delayed Birth Certificate filed with the state registrar June 19, 1957.

12. Location of Birth: Co.: Northumberland; District: Heathsville; Town: Lara.
    Full Name of Child: Marvin Meade **Hinton**.
    Date of Birth: August 15, 1919.
    Father's Name: Ira David Hinton, age: 36, occupation: farming.
    Race: White.
    Mother's Maiden Name: Ida Byrd Thomas, age: 36.
    Race: White.
    Original Birth Certificate filed in Northumberland County October 9, 1919.

---

[66] Although the location of this birth is given as Farnham, Farnham is in Richmond County, VA.

13. Location of Birth: Co.: Northumberland; District: not given; Town: Alfonso.[67]
Full Name of Child: Claudia Lucile **Jett**.
Date of Birth: January 31, 1907.
Father's Name: Wylie Pursell Jett, age: 37, occupation: farmer.
Race: White.
Margaret Maiden Name: Sallie Jane Harris, age: 38.
Race: White.
Delayed Birth Certificate filed with the state registrar April 23, 1956.[68]

14. Location of Birth: Co.: Northumberland; District: Heathsville; Town: Miskimon.
Full Name of Child: Howard Norman **Jones**.
Date of Birth: January 24, 1913.
Father's Name: John Howard Jones, age: 23, occupation: farmer.
Race: White.
Mother's Maiden Name: Easter Priscilla Norman, age: 19.
Race: White.
Original Birth Certificate filed in Northumberland County November 10, 1913.

15. Location of Birth: Co.: Northumberland; District: not given; Town: Rehoboth Church.
Full Name of Child: Asbury Pinkard **Joyner**.
Date of Birth: November 19, 1905.
Father's Name: Wilmer Joyner, age: 30, occupation: government clerk.
Race: White.
Mother's Maiden Name: Lena Kelley Pinkard, age: 30.
Race: White.
Delayed Birth Certificate filed with the state registrar November 7, 1939.

16. Location of Birth: Co.: Northumberland; District: Heathsville, Town: Miskimon.
Full Name of Child: Hilda Irene **Mahan**.[69]
Date of Birth: August 17, 1918.
Father's Name: Frank Mahan, age: 30, occupation: day laborer.
Race: White.
Mother's Maiden Name: Annie May McNeal, age: 19.
Race: White.
Original Birth Certificate filed in Northumberland County with the August report in 1918.

---

[67] Although the location of this birth is given as Alfonso, Alfonso is in Lancaster County, VA.

[68] In the left-hand margin of this birth certificate, it states, "Taken from my records. C. T. Peirce."

[69] At the bottom of this birth certificate, it states, "Given name added from a supplemental report." It is dated September 10, 1918 and signed J. T. Beane.

17. Location of Birth: Co.: Northumberland; District: not given; Town: Miskimon.
Full Name of Child: Joseph David **Marsh**.
Date of Birth: July 30, 1913.
Father's Name: Wayland Joseph Marsh, age: 29, occupation: farmer.
Race: White.
Mother's Maiden Name: Julia Effy Dawson, age: 29.
Race: White.
Original Birth Certificate filed in Northumberland County September 10, 1913.

18. Location of Birth: Co.: Northumberland; District: Heathsville; Town: Miskimon.
Full Name of Child: Myrtis Elma **Marsh**.[70]
Date of Birth: August 20, 1918.
Father's Name: W. J. Marsh, age: 34, occupation: farmer.
Race: White.
Mother's Maiden Name: Julia Dawson, age: 34.
Race: White.
Original Birth Certificate filed in Northumberland County August, 1918.

19. Location of Birth: Co.: Northumberland; District: Heathsville; Town: Miskimon.
Full Name of Child: Lester Gray **Sampson**.[71]
Date of Birth: December 29, 1916.
Father's Name: Frank K. Sampson, age: 32, occupation: farmer.
Race: White.
Mother's Maiden Name: Gertrude Cockrell, age: 28.
Race: White.
Original Birth Certificate filed in Northumberland County February 10, 1917.

20. Location of Birth: Co.: Northumberland; District: Heathsville; Town: Miskimon.
Full Name of Child: Thomas Weston **Sampson**.[72]
Date of Birth: November 12, 1912.
Father's Name: Frank K. Sampson, age: 27, occupation: merchant.
Race: White.
Mother's Maiden Name: Lillian G. Cockrell, age: 24.
Race: White.
Original Birth Certificate filed in Northumberland County filed November, 1912.

---

[70] At the bottom of this birth certificate, it states, "Given name added from a supplemental report." This is dated September 10, 1918 and signed J. T. Beane.

[71] At the bottom of this birth certificate, it states, "Given name added from a supplemental report; List of names." This is dated January 12, 1942 and signed W. A. P., State Registrar.

[72] At the bottom of this birth certificate, it states, "Given name added from a supplemental record." It is dated January 30, 1913 and signed E. W. Eichelberger.

21. Location of Birth: Co.: Northumberland; District: not given; Town: Miskimon.
    Full Name of Child: Thornton Thomas **Sampson**.
    Date of Birth: July 13, 1911.
    Father's Name: Booker Hundley Sampson, age: 22, occupation: farmer.
    Race: White.
    Mother's Maiden Name: Lavenia Anne Cockrell, age: 21.
    Race: White.
    Delayed Birth Certificate filed with the state registrar June 26, 1956.

22. Location of Birth: Co.: Northumberland; District: Heathsville; Town: Lara.
    Full Name of Child: Millard Hue [possibly Hugh] **Thomas**.
    Date of Birth: August 23, 1919.
    Father's Name: Prince Albert Thomas, age: 31, occupation: farming.
    Race: White.
    Mother's Maiden Name: Evlyn [Evelyn] Ostelle [Estelle] Cockrell,[73] age: 33.
    Race: White.
    Original Birth Certificate filed in Northumberland County October 9, 1919.

23. Location of Birth: Co.: Northumberland; District: Heathsville, Town: Lara.
    Full Name of Child: Philip Wesley **Thomas**.[74]
    Date of Birth: May 15, 1913.
    Father's Name: Prince Albert Thomas, age: 25, occupation: merchant.
    Race: White.
    Mother's Maiden Name: Everlyn [Evelyn] Estelle Cockrell, age: 26.
    Race: White.
    Original Birth Certificate filed in Northumberland County June 10, 1913.

---

[73] Correct spelling of Evelyn Estelle Cockrell's name comes from Ed Cockrell, *The Miskimon Cockrells*, p. 30, self-published 2007.

[74] At the bottom of this birth certificate, it states "Given name added from registrant's affidavit and attending physician's records." It is dated September 19, 1961.

RICHMOND COUNTY, VIRGINIA, HOME BIRTHS ATTENDED BY DR. C. T. PEIRCE

1900 to 1919

All information and spellings are as they appear on the birth certificates. All Birth records are listed in alphabetical order. Race is listed as it appears on the birth certificate.[75]

1. Location of Birth: Co.: Richmond; District: Farnham; Town: not given.
   Full Name of Child: Allwin Rice **Barrack**.[76]
   Date of Birth: June 18, 1918.
   Father's Name: C. M. Barrack, age: 34, occupation: merchant.
   Race: White.
   Mother's Maiden Name: Florence Rice, age: 28.
   Race: White.
   Original Birth Certificate filed in Richmond County August 28, 1918.

2. Location of Birth: Co.: Richmond; District: Farnham; Town: Downings.
   Full Name of Child: Lurline Maria **Barrack**.
   Date of Birth: March 4, 1915.
   Father's Name: J. O. Barrack, age: 39, occupation: farmer.
   Race: White.
   Mother's Maiden Name: Susie Benson, age: 30.
   Race: White.
   Original Birth Certificate filed in Richmond County March 29, 1915.

3. Location of Birth: Co.: Richmond; District: Farnham, Town: Downings.
   Full Name of Child: Grace Emma **Bryant**.
   Date of Birth: September 6, 1915.
   Father's Name: J. C. Bryant, age: 36, occupation: sawmiller.
   Race: White.
   Mother's Maiden Name: Emma Revere, age: 35.
   Race: White.
   Original Birth Certificate filed in Richmond County October 9, 1915.

---

[75] Source for all images of birth certificates is Ancestry.com, *Virginia, U.S., Birth Records, 1912-2015, Delayed Birth Records, 1721-1920* [Original data: Virginia, Births, 1721–2015, Virginia Department of Health, Richmond, Virginia], accessed 2021-2022.

[76] At the bottom of the birth certificate, it states, "Given name added from a supplemental report, August 20, 1918. Mrs. S. J. Dodson [local registrar]."

4. Location of Birth: Co.: Richmond; District: Farnham; Town: not given.
    Full Name of Child: Robert Charles **Bryant**.[77]
    Date of Birth: May 26, 1917.
    Father's Name: Otis Bryant, age: 24, occupation: farmer.
    Race: White.
    Mother's Maiden Name: Evelyn Douglas, age: 20.
    Race: White.
    Original Birth Certificate filed in Richmond County June 18, 1917.

5. Location of Birth: Co.: Richmond; District: Farnham; Town: Simonsons.
    Full Name of Child: Annette Bryant **Corson**.
    Date of Birth: June 6, 1915.
    Father's Name: Alfred L. Corson, age: 32, occupation: farmer.
    Race: White.
    Mother's Maiden Name: Mary Bryant, age: 40.
    Race: White.
    Original Birth Certificate filed in Richmond County June 18, 1915.

6. Location of Birth: Co.: Richmond; District: Farnham; Town: Downings.
    Full Name of Child: Esther Margarett **Davenport**.
    Date of Birth: February 25, 1915.
    Father's Name: Vernon Davenport, age: 29, occupation: farmer.
    Race: White.
    Mother's Maiden Name: Annie Rice, age: 20.
    Race: White.
    Original Birth Certificate filed in Richmond County March 29, 1915.

7. Location of Birth: Co.: Richmond; District: Farnham; Town: Farnham.
    Full Name of Child: William Howard **Davenport**.
    Date of Birth: November 15, 1917.
    Father's Name: C. T. Davenport, age: 21, occupation: farmer.
    Race: White.
    Mother's Maiden Name: Gertrude Alice Davenport, age: 17.
    Race: White.
    Delayed Birth Certificate filed August 6, 1932.[78]

8. Location of Birth: Co.: Richmond; District: not given; Town: Farnham.
    Full Name of Child: Bradford Manuel **Dunaway**.
    Date of Birth: July 28, 1917.
    Father's Name: Thomas Samuel Dunaway, age: 49, occupation: farmer.
    Race: White.
    Mother's Maiden Name: Eunice Ann Sydnor, age: 29.
    Race: White.
    Delayed Birth Certificate filed with the deputy state registrar December 15, 1941.

---

[77] At the bottom of the birth certificate, it states, "#2 name added by marriage record & affidavit September 20, 1978." This is followed by the initials J R. The word "Amended" is written at the top of the birth certificate.

[78] At the top of this birth certificate is written "Card Sent September 7, 1932."

9. Location of Birth: Co.: Richmond; District: Farnham; Town: Farnham.
   Full Name of Child: Walter Peirce **Dunaway**.
   Date of Birth: January 24, 1912.
   Father's Name: T. S. Dunaway, age: 45, occupation: farming.
   Race: White.
   Mother's Maiden Name: Eunice Ann Sydnor, age: 25.
   Race: White.
   Delayed Birth Certificate filed March 5, 1940. Card sent March 14, 1940.

10. Location of Birth: Co.: Richmond; District: Farnham; Town: Farnham.
    Full Name of Child: Wharton Claybrook **Dunaway**.
    Date of Birth: July 10, 1917.
    Father's Name: J. C. Dunaway, age: 27, occupation: farmer.
    Race: White.
    Mother's Maiden Name: Eunice Irene Davenport, age: 29.
    Race: White.
    Delayed Birth Certificate filed August 1, 1932. Card sent September 7, 1932.

11. Location of Birth: Co.: Richmond; District: not given; Town: Farnham.
    Full Name of Child: William Asa **Dunaway**.
    Date of Birth: March 25, 1918.
    Father's Name: William Kirk Dunaway, age: 41, occupation: farmer.
    Race: White.
    Mother's Maiden Name: Cora Ann Davenport, age: 25.
    Race: White.
    Delayed Birth Certificate filed with the deputy state registrar December 1, 1941.

12. Location of Birth: Co.: Richmond; District: Farnham; Town: Downings.
    Full Name of Child: Richard S. **Hinton**.
    Date of Birth: November 26, 1913.
    Father's Name: Newton R. Hinton, age: 26, occupation: farmer.
    Race: White.
    Mother's Maiden Name: Edna Bean, age: 23.
    Race: White.
    Original Birth Certificate filed in Richmond County January 6, 1914.

13. Location of Birth: Co.: Richmond; District: Farnham; Town: Robley.
    Full Name of Child: Sherwood Lawless **Lowery**.
    Date of Birth: November 11, 1915.
    Father's Name: J. L. Lowery, age: 37, occupation: salesman.
    Race: White.
    Mother's Maiden Name: L. D. McKenney, age: 26.
    Race: White.
    Delayed Birth Certificate filed March 1, 1931. Card sent April 9, 1931.

14. Location of Birth: Co.: Richmond; District: not given; Town: Lara.
    Full Name of Child: Eunice Eva **Rice**.
    Date of Birth: December 26, 1907.
    Father's Name: Thomas James Rice, age: 32, occupation: farmer.
    Race: White.
    Mother's Maiden Name: Eva Naomi Gough, age: 29.
    Race: White.
    Delayed Birth Certificate filed with the state registrar November 12, 1958.

15. Location of Birth: Co.: Richmond; District: not given; Town: Lara.
    Full Name of Child: Mabel Anne **Rice**.
    Date of Birth: April 29, 1904.
    Father's Name: Thomas James Rice, age: 29, occupation: farmer.
    Race: White.
    Mother's Maiden Name: Eva Naomi Gough, age: 26.
    Race: White.
    Delayed Birth Certificate filed with the state registrar September 29, 1958.

16. Location of Birth: Co.: Richmond; District: not given; Town: Lara.
    Full Name of Child: Thomas Benton **Rice**.
    Date of Birth: June 10, 1906.
    Father's Name: Thomas James Rice, age: 31, occupation: farmer.
    Race: White.
    Mother's Maiden Name: Eva Naomi Gough, age: 28.
    Delayed Birth Certificate filed with the state registrar November 12, 1958.

17. In a letter from William Hugh **Rice** to the Bureau of Vital Statistics in Richmond, VA, dated May 12, 1942, he writes:

    "Gentlemen:

    Please furnish me with a copy of my birth certificate at the earliest possible date. The following is information pertaining to my birth:

    Date of Birth: March 22, 1915.
    Place of Birth: Richmond or Lancaster County.
    Name: William Hugh Rice
    Name of mother: Eva N. Rice.
    Name of father: Thomas J. Rice.
    Doctor presiding: Dr. C. T. Peirce

    It will be appreciated if you will comply with my request promptly as the matter is urgent. I will gladly send check by return mail to cover any charges.

    Very truly yours,
    William Hugh Rice
    [his signature]"[79]

[79] This compiler was not able to find a birth certificate for Mr. Rice on Ancestry.com. Ancestry just had this letter as a record of his birth. See the image on the following page, recorded as Certificate Number 1915011296 in *Virginia, U.S., Birth Records, 1912-2015, Delayed Birth Records, 1721-1920*.

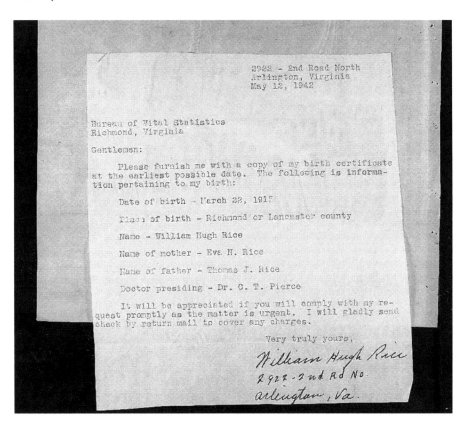

18. Location of Birth: Co.: Richmond; District: Farnham; Town: Lara.
    Full Name of Child: Andrew **Thomas**.
    Date of Birth: March 1, 1915.
    Father's Name: William Andrew Thomas, age: 38, occupation: day laborer.
    Race: White.
    Mother's Maiden Name: Mamie Corine Jones, age: 21.
    Race: White.
    Original Birth Certificate: March 29, 1915.

19. Location of Birth: Co.: Richmond; District: Farnham; Town: Lara.
    Full Name of Child: Theodore McKenley **Thomas**.
    Date of Birth: September 29, 1919.
    Father's Name: William Thomas, age: 42, occupation: farmer.
    Race: White.
    Mother's Maiden Name: Corine Jones, age: 25.
    Original Birth Certificate filed in Richmond County October 4, 1919.

20. Location of Birth: Co.: Richmond; District: not given; Town: Farnham.
Full Name of Child: William Marvin **Thomas**.
Date of Birth: January 31, 1917.
Father's Name: W. A. Thomas, age: 40, occupation: farmer.
Race: White.
Mother's Maiden Name: Mamie Corine Jones, age: 22.
Race: White.
Delayed Birth Certificate filed with the local registrar November 10, 1943.

21. Location of Birth: Co.: Richmond; District: Farnham; Town: Downings.
Full Name of Child: Agnes Omega **Whittaker**.
Date of Birth: September 13, 1916.
Father's Name: C. J. Whittaker, age: 44, occupation: farmer.
Race: White.
Mother's Maiden Name: Columbia Clark, age: 44.
Race: White.
Original Birth Certificate filed in Richmond County January 22, 1917.

INDEX TO BIRTH RECORDS ONLY

(Includes Children, Fathers, and Mothers)

Lancaster, Northumberland, Richmond Counties

LANCASTER COUNTY:

Adams
  Avelon, 35
Alford
  Florence Virginia, 11
  Henry Timothy, 11
Ashley
  Maude, 46
Ball
  Andrew, 12
  Calvin, 13
  Cora M., 12
  Fannie, 12
  Ford, 12
  Julia, 21
  Lucile, 12
  Maria, 17
  Mary Corline, 12
  Paul, 13
  Walter Oneal, 13
  Warner, 12
  William Ryland, 12, 13
Barker
  Earl Robertson, 13
  Sarah Lena, 48, 49
  W. J., 13
Barnes
  Fannie Louise, 23
  Fleet Everett, 13
  Thomas, 13
Barrack
  Addie Kate, 16
  Christine/Christy Carrie, 19
  Clara Sarah, 18
  Clarence Eugene, Jr., 13
  Clarence Eugene, Sr., 13
  Edwin Taylor, 14
  Robert, 14

Bartlett
  Eliza Virginia, 31
Barton
  Alva Floyd, 14
  Julian J., Jr., 14
  Julian J., Sr., 14
  Raymond Alexander, 14
Bass
  Rosser Lee, 14
  Thomas Albert, 14
Beane
  Edna, 32
Belfield
  Clementine, 45
Bell
  N. Kay, 21
Boothe
  Ila B., 36
Boyd
  Alice, 18
  Elnora, 15
  Lillie, 27, 28
  Nathaniel, 15
  Neomi, 15
  Selman, 15
Branham
  Ada, 44
Bromley
  Edward, 15
  Grace Garnett, 15
Brooks
  Annie Street, 15
  Extra, 15
  Extra Dorsey, 15
  Harriet, 33, 34
  Robert, 15
  Victoria, 16

Brown
 Armon, 16
 Bessie Alvey, 48
 Charles, 16
 Charles Monroe, 16
 Laura Jenette, 22
 Monnie Helen, 16
 William Henry, 16
Bruer
 Janie, 43
Bush
 Effus Claybrook, 18, 19
 Fannie, 31
Cambel
 Eliza, 51
Cannon,
 Gertrude, 45
Carter
 Bessie, 34
 Eddie, 17
 Eugene, Jr., 17
 Eugene, Sr., 17
 F. P., 17
 George Albert, 17
 Gilbert, 17
 James Henry, 17
 Lumbard, 17
 Rosa, 32, 33
 Rufus, 18
 Sprig, 18
Chilton
 Bratton Leroy, 18
 Fannie Jones, 27
 Robert, 18
Chowning
 Charles Fairfax, 18
 Eunice Elizabeth, 18
 James Hancock, 18
 Lucy, 52
Clark
 Clarence William, 19
 Clyde B., 19
 Edward Carlyle Davis, 18
 Elizabeth Louise, 19
 Elsie Graham, 19
 Genevieve Pearl, 19
 Homer Butts, 19
 L.R., 18
 Lewis Ryland, 19
 Sydnor Bernard, 19
 Thomas Hodges, 19

Cockrill
 Clinton Stark, 20
 D. W., 20
Coleman
 Adelia, 20
 Lewis, 20
 Priscilla, 26
Combs
 Elizabeth Edrington, 39
Conaway
 Grace, 52
 Lawrence, 20
 Louis, 20
Conrad
 Emil, 20
 John, 20
 Lottie Stella Peirce, 20
Conway
 Maggie, 21
 Robert, 21
Corbin
 Milburn James, 21
 Sam, 21
Coulbourn
 Alma, 33
Cox
 Mary Lelia, 30
Crockett
 Mary Ellen, 19
Croxton
 James H., 21
 James Henry, 51
 Thomas Loyd, 21
 Unnamed baby girl, 51
Curren
 Maggie, 20
Curry
 Bertina, 53
Dardwell
 Laura, 54
Davenport
 Hidie, 21, 51
 Howard, 52
 Luther James, 21
 Raney, 52
 Sarah Elizabeth, 40
 Unnamed baby boy, 52
 Unnamed baby girl, 51, 52

NORTHUMBERLAND COUNTY:

Beane
    George Hinton, 55
    George Milton, 55
    Mary Gertrude, 55
    T. S., 55
Bee
    Ida, 55
    Unnamed baby boy, 55
Cannon
    Lessie/Lusie Gertrude, 56
Cockrell
    Evelyn Estelle, 60
    Lavenia Anne, 60
    Lillian Gertrude, 59
Davenport
    A. B., 56
    James Everett, 56
    John Webster, 56
    W. B., 56
    William Ray, 56
Dawson
    Julia Effy, 59
Edwards
    Sarah Ann, 56
    William Corbin, 56
Forrester
    Elgin W., 57
    Elton James, 57
    Ivis Lee, 57
    Ivis Leonard, 57
Gill
    Mary Alice, 57
Hall
    Janie Gray, 55
Harris
    Sallie Jane, 58
    William Richard, Jr., 57
    William Richard, Sr., 57
Hinton
    Grace, 55
    Ira D., 57
    Margaret Virginia, 57
    Marvin Meade, 57
Jett
    Claudia Lucile, 58
    Wylie Pursell, 58
Jones
    Howard Norman, 58
    John Howard, 58

Joyner
    Asbury Pinkard, 58
    Wilmer, 58
Luttrell
    Mary Elizabeth, 56
Mahan
    Frank, 58
    Hilda Irene, 58
Marsh
    Joseph David, 59
    Myrtis Elma, 59
    Wayland Joseph, 59
McNeal
    Annie May, 58
Norman
    Easter Priscilla, 58
Pinkard
    Lena Kelley, 58
Revere
    Nannie Cora, 57
Rice
    Sofia Anne, 56
Sampson
    Booker Hundley, 60
    Frank K., 59
    Lester Gray, 59
    Thomas Weston, 59
    Thornton Thomas, 60
Thomas
    Eva Katherine, 57
    Ida Byrd, 57
    Millard Hugh, 60
    Philip Wesley, 60
    Prince Albert, Sr., 60

Made in the USA
Columbia, SC
23 June 2023

18708869R00050